STACEY AND THE MYSTERY
OF STONEYBROOK

Other books by
Ann M. Martin

Rachel Parker, Kindergarten Show-off
Eleven Kids, One Summer
Ma and Pa Dracula
Yours Turly, Shirley
Ten Kids, No Pets
Slam Book
Just a Summer Romance
Missing Since Monday
With You and Without You
Me and Katie (the Pest)
Stage Fright
Inside Out
Bummer Summer

BABY-SITTERS LITTLE SISTER series
THE BABY-SITTERS CLUB mysteries
THE BABY-SITTERS CLUB series

STACEY AND THE MYSTERY OF STONEYBROOK

Ann M. Martin

AN
APPLE
PAPERBACK

SCHOLASTIC INC.
New York Toronto London Auckland Sydney

*The author gratefully acknowledges
Ellen Miles
for her help in
preparing this manuscript.*

Cover art by Hodges Soileau

ISBN 0-590-73284-6

12 11 10 9 8 7 6 5 4 3 2   5   7 8 9/9 0 1/0

Printed in the U.S.A.   40

CHAPTER 1

As the train started up, I sat back in my seat, leaned my head against the window, and smiled to myself. On the surface it might seem as if I, eighth-grader Stacey McGill, had the perfect life. Most of the time I live in lovely old Stoneybrook, Connecticut. That's where my train was headed. I go to a great school, have tons of friends, and belong to the best club in the world — but more about that later.

Every now and then, though — pretty much whenever I feel like it — I get to go on a "Fun-Filled Action-Packed All-Expenses-Paid-Weekend in the Glamorous Big Apple, New York City!" as they say on the game shows.

That's how it looks on the surface. And, I'll admit, I *had* just had a terrific weekend in New York. But as soon as you peek beneath the surface of my life, you'll see that it isn't quite as ideal as it looks. Maybe you've guessed by now that the reason I go back and forth be-

1

tween Stoneybrook and New York is that my parents are divorced. When they broke up, my mom and I moved to Stoneybrook, and my dad stayed in the city. The split happened pretty recently, and believe me, it was not Fun-Filled, although it was kind of Action-Packed. Before they split up, my parents fought a lot — not physically or anything, but all that yelling really got to me.

How did my mom and I end up in Stoneybrook? Well, that's kind of complicated, but here goes. I grew up in New York City, and in a way I'll always consider it my home. I love all the excitement. I also love eating out, going to shows, and . . . shopping! There's no place like New York for great clothes. I still shop there, which means I look pretty sophisticated in Stoneybrook. For example, I had dressed for my train ride in a white jumpsuit, layered over a blue tank top. I had on white push-down socks with blue hearts all over them, a wide blue patent leather belt, and a wild necklace made of all kinds of plastic sea creatures in a rainbow of colors.

Oops. I think I got off the track there a little. Where was I? Okay, so I grew up in New York, but then when I was in seventh grade my dad's company transferred him to their Connecticut office. And then, a year later, just as

I'd really begun to feel at home in Stoneybrook, they transferred him *back* to New York. Can you believe it?

It wasn't long after we'd moved back to the city that I noticed how my parents seemed to be fighting all the time. And you can guess the rest of the story. *They* decided to get divorced, *I* decided to move back to Stoneybrook with my mom (instead of moving to the Upper East Side with my dad), and that's why I was on that train, thinking about my weekend in New York.

The first great thing about the weekend was that my dad had taken the whole day off on Saturday just to be with me. I know, you're thinking, What's the big deal? Nobody works on Saturday. Nobody except my dad. I guess he's what you'd call a workaholic. That was one of the things he and my mom used to fight about: how his job was more important to him than his family, how he was never home. . . . But on *this* Saturday, I guess it was important to him to show me a good time, because that's what he did.

We started the day by going out to brunch, to this little café I've always loved. All the waiters are really cute, and you can get any kind of omelette you want. The food is excellent, but what I really love is the cappuccino.

(That's coffee with foamy hot milk in it and cinnamon sprinkled on top. Yum.) I'm not usually allowed to drink coffee, but my dad always lets me have a little of his cappuccino.

After brunch we just walked around for awhile, window shopping and people watching. You never know who or what you'll see in New York. At one point, as we were crossing Fifth Avenue, I looked to my right just in time to see Gary Rockman (he is the hottest — and most gorgeous — star around right now) jump into a cab. I nearly died!

My dad knows that one of my favorite stores is Fiorucci, so when we got near it he suggested that we go in. He told me to pick out anything I wanted. For a second, I considered taking him at his word and asking him to buy me this outrageous purple suede jacket. Was it beautiful! Cropped short at the waist and covered with fringe all up the arms and across the back. But I did the mature thing (silly me!) and picked out a wild pair of sunglasses — heart-shaped ones, in a black-and-white checkerboard pattern. Claudia (my best friend in Stoneybrook) will love them, I know.

We walked and shopped some more, and by 5:00 we were starving, so we decided to go out for dinner. Dad let me choose the restaurant, so I picked Hunan Supreme, this Chinese place in our old neighborhood. We know the owner there, Mr. Lee, and the food is great.

Our meal was delicious, but I have to say that dinner was not my favorite part of the weekend. Here's why: When our food came, I started to dig in, but Dad just sat there looking worried.

"Are you sure those noodles are okay for you to eat, honey?" he asked.

That might seem like a silly question, but he actually had a good reason to ask it. I'm a diabetic. I have to be really careful about what I eat, when I eat it, and how many calories it has. If I'm not careful, my blood sugar gets all out of whack, and I can get seriously ill. I also have to take insulin every day. I give myself the shots, which sounds horrible, but it really is no big deal once you get used to it. When I first got diabetes, my parents were constantly fussing over me. They made me nuts. But by now they basically know that I know how to take care of myself.

Unfortunately, though, I'd recently been told by my regular doctor that I'd have to be even *more* careful with my diet and with taking just the right amount of insulin. I guess my body is going through some changes right now that make it hard for everything to stay in balance.

So there I was, about to take another bite of my noodles. I *do* know that they're okay for me to eat, of course; otherwise I'd never have ordered them. Who wants to get sick? Then my dad spoke up again.

"I think you should schedule an appointment with Dr. Werner for the next time you visit me."

Dr. Werner is my diabetes specialist. I don't have to see her regularly — just when there's a special problem.

I hate it when my parents start worrying about my diabetes. I don't feel sick all the time, and I can't stand being treated like an invalid. To tell you the truth, it scares me a little when they make a federal case out of my diabetes. It reminds me that I do have a serious illness.

"Dad, it's under control. Come on! Don't you think I know how to take care of myself? I'm a big girl now, remember? I'm not your little boontsie anymore." ("Boontsie" is what my dad calls kids who are at that really cute big-tummy, bowlegged stage, around two or three.)

He softened. I could tell I'd put off having to see Dr. Werner for awhile, anyway.

"No, you're not my little boontsie anymore, are you, Anastasia?"

He's the only one who gets away with calling me that. I know, it *is* my real name, but really. Anastasia?

So that was my big weekend in New York. On Sunday I woke up late in my dad's apartment. I could hear him clicking away at his computer keyboard in the room next to mine. I should have known he couldn't stand to take the *whole* weekend off. I started to get a little mad at him — after all, it *was* Sunday — but just then the doorbell rang.

I threw on my bathrobe and ran for the door. It was my best-friend-in-New-York, Laine Cummings, carrying a huge, bulging bag from Zabar's. Zabar's is only the most incredible deli in the world. Everybody goes there on Sunday mornings to get bagels, fresh cream cheese, and all kinds of other goodies.

Laine and I pulled everything out of the bag, arranged it on the table, and proceeded to eat and gossip until it was time for me to catch my train.

I'd just started thinking again about that purple jacket, when the conductor came strolling through the car.

"Stoneybrook, all for Stoneybrook, get off here!" he said.

I jumped off the last step of the train right into my mother's arms. She gave me a huge hug.

"I've missed you so much, sweetie! How was your weekend?"

As we walked to the car, got in, and started home, I gave her a blow-by-blow account of my visit to New York. As she listened to the details of that wonderful Saturday I could see her mouth tighten a little.

"Do you mean to tell me that he *really* took the entire weekend off?" she asked. "I can't believe it."

I hadn't told her about the computer sounds that morning, but I didn't want to go into it now, even though I could see that I hadn't made her feel so great by telling her all about the terrific time I had.

"Mom, I missed you, too. Let's go into the city together sometime soon. Remember how much fun we used to have in the cosmetics department at Bloomingdale's?"

She laughed. I'll bet she was thinking of the day we tried on at least fourteen different types of perfume each.

As soon as we pulled into the driveway, I ran up to my room to unpack. It was good to be back — after all, Stoneybrook is really my home for now. After dinner, I called Claud to tell her about my weekend.

"Oh, Stace, I can't believe you didn't at least *try* for the jacket!" she cried. (Claudia loves clothes as much as I do. Maybe even more.)

"But wait'll you see my sunglasses. They're to die for, I'm telling you."

We talked for awhile until my mom called up the stairs to let me know that it was time to get off the phone.

" 'Bye Stace! See you in school tomorrow," said Claudia.

"And at the meeting, too," I reminded her.

Claudia and I, along with our other Stoneybrook-best-friends (all five of them!) belong to the Baby-sitters Club. The club is really a business — a baby-sitting business, of course — but I'll tell you more about it later.

As soon as I hung up the phone, I headed up to bed. I was beat! Those "Fun-Filled Action-Packed Weekends" sure can take a lot out of you.

CHAPTER 2

I'd been planning to walk over to Claudia's for the Baby-sitters Club meeting the next day, but for some reason I'd been running late from the second I got up that morning. I guess I'm not used to going back and forth between my two "worlds" — New York and Stoneybrook. It takes me awhile to readjust every time I come back from a weekend away.

I started out the day by oversleeping. I gobbled my breakfast, threw on any old outfit I could find (the same white jumpsuit with a *pink* shirt and — oops! — red socks), and practically ran all the way to school. It seemed as though I was rushing around all day, and now here it was, almost 5:30, club meeting time, and I was still at home.

I grabbed my bike and hopped on. I knew I could still make it on time if I pedaled fast. As I rode, I thought about everyone I would see over at Claud's. I'd really been lucky to find so many great friends when I moved to Stoneybrook. If it hadn't been for the Baby-sitters Club, my life would sure be different.

The BSC was all Kristy's idea. That's Kristy Thomas, president of the club. She's always coming up with excellent ideas, but this one has to be the best.

It all started at the beginning of seventh grade. At the time, Kristy lived with her mom; her two older brothers, Sam and Charlie; and her little brother, David Michael. Her mom was divorced: Kristy's dad walked out on the family years ago. Kristy never even sees him. Isn't that awful? I thought my parents' divorce was the pits, but at least I get to *see* my dad pretty often.

Anyway, Kristy and her brothers used to baby-sit for David Michael most of the time, but when they couldn't, Mrs. Thomas would have to make a ton of phone calls to try to line up a sitter. One night as her mom was doing this, Kristy had one of her Brilliant Brainstorms. What if parents could reach a whole bunch of experienced sitters with just one call?

And so the Baby-sitters Club was born. Kristy got together with Claudia, as well as Mary Anne, who lived across the street and was Kristy's best friend. They immediately decided that they needed more than three people in the club, so Claud suggested me. We had met in school and were already becoming friends. Claudia was elected vice-president, mainly because we hold our meetings in her room. Plus she has her own phone with a private line — very important for the club. Mary Anne became secretary because she's neat and organized, and I took on the office of treasurer, because I'm good at math. We'd meet three times a week, on Mondays, Wednesdays, and Fridays. During our meetings parents would call us to line up sitters.

The club has worked perfectly since Day One, but believe me, it has been through some major changes, and so have all its members. I'm not the only one who feels like my whole life has been turned inside out and upside down in the last year or so. Also, the BSC has grown a lot since it started. Besides the original members, there're now also Dawn, Jessi, and Mallory. Not to mention Logan and Shannon . . . but I'm getting ahead of myself here.

Let me go back to Kristy. Besides being brilliant, Kristy can also be bossy at times, and occasionally (I hate to say it) a little babyish. Kristy's small for her age and is kind of a tomboy. She wears the same thing every day: jeans, a turtleneck, a sweater, and running shoes. But Kristy's all right. She's had a crazy year or so, and I'd have to say she's dealing with it really well.

While Kristy was starting the club, her mom was falling in love with a real, true millionaire named Watson Brewer. They got married, and Kristy moved across town to live in his — get this — mansion. She wasn't crazy about Watson *or* the move at first, but she did like Watson's kids, her new stepbrother and stepsister, Andrew and Karen. And just as the two families were starting to become one, Kristy's mom and Mr. Brewer decided to adopt Emily Michelle, a two-year-old Vietnamese girl. (She's *adorable*.) And then Kristy's grandmother, Nannie, moved in to help take care of Emily! So it's a pretty full house right now, especially when you throw in Shannon, the Bernese mountain dog puppy, and Boo-Boo, the fat, mean, geriatric cat. But they all seem to be getting along well, and Kristy likes her new house, new family, and new neighborhood better all the time.

As I mentioned before, Claudia Kishi (my best friend, remember?) is the vice-president of the club. Claudia is, well . . . *gorgeous*. She's Japanese-American and has L-O-N-G silky black hair, a perfect complexion (despite her incurable junk-food habit), and almond-shaped eyes. And if there's anyone in town who's a wilder, more sophisticated dresser than me, it's got to be Claud. She's a really talented artist, and she's always putting together the most outrageous outfits, then accessorizing them with even more outrageous jewelry, which, of course, she's made herself.

Claud's likes and dislikes? Likes: reading Nancy Drew mysteries. Dislikes: studying. Has a love/hate relationship with her genius older sister, Janine. Misses: her grandmother Mimi, whom she was really close to. Mimi died not long ago and actually we *all* miss her.

Mary Anne Spier, the club secretary, has brown hair and brown eyes, just like Kristy. But while Kristy is loudmouthed and always in the spotlight, Mary Anne is extremely shy and sensitive. (And I mean *sensitive*. She cries at the drop of a hat — probably because she feels sorry for the poor hat!) Mary Anne grew up with just her father. Her mom died when she was really little. For years, Mr. Spier was incredibly strict with Mary Anne, but he's finally begun to loosen up. He even let her get a kitten!

If there's anybody, besides her father, that Mary Anne loves more than Tigger (that's her kitten), it's her boyfriend, Logan Bruno. I always think it's kind of weird that Mary Anne, who is the shyest girl in the Baby-sitters Club, is the only one of us who has a steady boyfriend. I guess Logan must like Mary Anne for the same reasons all of us do: She's understanding, a good listener, and really a lot of fun.

Mary Anne is another one who's had a major change in her life recently, but before I go into that, let me tell you about Dawn Schafer, since she's got something to do with that change.

Dawn is the alternate officer of the club, which means that she can fill in for any of the other officers if they can't make it to a meeting. (She was treasurer the whole time I was living in New York.) Dawn moved here from California when her parents got a divorce. Her mom had grown up here, so it was natural that she'd want to come back. Their first year in Stoneybrook was kind of rough. Dawn's little brother, Jeff, didn't adjust well to the move. He never stopped missing his dad and feeling homesick for California. So finally, he moved back there to live with his dad. I know Dawn misses him a lot. But she's really close to her mom, and she loves the house they live in — it was built in 1795 and it has a secret passage and maybe even a real ghost. Honest.

Even though she's lived here for almost two

years now, Dawn still looks like a California girl. She dresses like a true individual, and she's got long, long pale blonde hair and beautiful blue eyes. She's into health food in a major way, and it doesn't seem to bother her at all when we all make gagging noises at her tofu salads. Dawn just is who she is: She's got a lot of self-confidence and she doesn't seem to care too much about what other people think.

Now, remember when I said that Dawn had something to do with the big change in Mary Anne's life? Well, get this: Dawn's mother recently got married. Who did she marry? Mary Anne's father! Can you believe it? They used to date each other in high school when they were growing up, right here in Stoneybrook. Then, when Mrs. Schafer moved back here, the romance began all over again.

So Dawn and Mary Anne are now stepsisters! And I can't say that the transition from friends to relatives was an easy one for them. When Mary Anne, her father, and Tigger first moved into Dawn's house, things were more than a little rocky for awhile. But it seems as if they're all getting along much better now.

Okay, there are still two more members of the club, our junior officers, Mallory Pike and Jessi Ramsey. They were both asked to join while I was away in New York last year and the other members couldn't quite keep up with all the jobs they were offered. Of course, they're still members even though I'm back now. They're called junior officers because they're two years younger than the rest of us — they're in sixth grade — and aren't allowed to sit at night, except for their own brothers and sisters. But there are plenty of day jobs to keep them busy. Mallory and Jessi are both great sitters, and we were lucky to get them for the club.

Mallory's a good sitter partly because she comes from a huge family. She has seven younger sisters and brothers! The Pikes have always been major clients of ours — Mal is actually someone we used to sit for. But she was a big help even then, and now she's grown up a lot. She knows just about everything about kids — she's seen it all!

Mal loves to read and write — in fact, she's thinking of becoming a children's book author someday. Her favorite books to read are horse stories. I think she's read *Misty of Chincoteague* something like seventy-six times!

Mal's main problem is being eleven. That's right, being eleven. She feels more grown-up than her parents are ready to let her be. (That's a funny way to put it, but you know what I

17

mean.) She wants to get contacts, instead of wearing glasses, and she hates her braces with a passion. At least her parents finally let her get her hair cut and her ears pierced. As for the rest, I guess she'll just have to be patient. That's easy to say, but I know how hard that can be.

Mallory's best friend is, guess who, Jessi Ramsey. They became best friends almost right away, when Jessi's family moved here last year. I guess Mal really needed somebody right then, and I *know* Jessi did. Her family had a hard time when they first moved to Stoneybrook. Why? Because they're black, and there are hardly any other black families in town. I know, it shouldn't make a difference *what* color someone is, but it did to a lot of people. It was so unfair! I think things are better for the Ramseys now. Jessi's little sister, Becca (short for Rebecca), has a best friend, and her baby brother, Squirt (his real name is John Philip Ramsey, Jr., but Squirt fits him much better), would be happy anywhere. Plus, the neighbors have seen that the Ramseys are simply a very nice family. By the way, guess where Jessi lives — in my old house!

Jessi loves horse stories, too, but her real passion is ballet. Jessi's a really talented dancer, and she puts a ton of work into practicing.

She takes lessons twice a week in Stamford, and believe me, they're *serious* lessons.

So, that's everyone. Oops! I almost forgot to mention our two associate members, Logan Bruno (Mary Anne's boyfriend) and Shannon Kilbourne, a friend of Kristy's from her new neighborhood. They don't come to meetings, but they are available to fill in for us when we have too many jobs to handle ourselves.

Whew! I think that's really everyone. What a crew! As I wheeled my bike into Claud's driveway, I glanced at my watch. Only minutes to spare. I would make it on time after all.

CHAPTER 3

I pounded up the stairs, out of breath. Had I made it? Just as I got to the door of Claud's room, I heard Kristy's voice.

"And then, on top of everything, Shannon got into the garbage. I walk into the kitchen and I see coffee grounds and chicken bones all over the floor!"

"Ew! You're kidding! Oh, ew." That was Mary Anne. I had a feeling that Kristy was talking about Shannon the puppy, not Shannon the Associate Member of the Baby-sitters Club.

Club meetings always start at five-thirty on the dot, as soon as Claud's digital clock flips over from five twenty-nine. The clock read five twenty-eight, so I had arrived in plenty of time. I settled onto Claud's bed next to Mary Anne, who was talking to Dawn. (Dawn was sitting backward in Claud's desk chair.) They were in the middle of an intense discussion regarding the exact color of Cam Geary's eyes, Cam Geary being Mary Anne's favorite star.

Most of Claudia was inside her closet. She was poking her hand into every compartment of her shoe bag. I had an idea of what she might be looking for, and sure enough, when she finally backed out of the closet, she was gripping a bag of M&M's in one hand and a package of Twinkies in the other. Plus she had a Twix bar clenched between her teeth. Claudia's parents, as you might guess, don't exactly approve of her junk-food habit, so she has to stash the stuff all over her room.

I was bursting with all the things I'd done on the weekend. I couldn't wait to tell everyone about how I'd spotted Gary Rockman, but Mallory grabbed their attention first.

"Did you guys see that old house at the end of Elm Street? They're tearing it down!"

That was my street. She must mean the other end, though, *away* from Claudia's house. There weren't all that many really old houses down at this end. But what was the big deal about a house being torn down? I started to say something about Gary Rockman, but Claud interrupted me.

"You're kidding! They're demolishing that

old place? I thought it was some kind of historical landmark. I thought they *couldn't* tear it down."

"I heard that some company wants to build condos there and got around that rule somehow," chimed in Mary Anne. "That house is the only one still standing in that whole area, and they're not about to let it get in their way."

I couldn't believe how fascinated everyone was with the "news" about some dumb old house. I guess that's what happens when you live in Stoneybrook all your life. *Anything* seems exciting.

"Order," said Kristy just then, making all of us jump. I looked at the clock. Sure enough. Five-thirty had just clicked into place. Kristy sat, as usual, in the director's chair. She wore her visor (I guess it makes her feel presidential), and she had a pencil stuck over her ear.

Kristy does a great job as president of the club, I must say. Dawn's always kind of wishing that Kristy would miss a meeting sometime — then, as alternate officer, Dawn would get to be president-for-a-day. But it's never happened yet. It's hard to imagine Kristy missing a meeting, and it's even harder to imagine anyone else as president.

"Has everyone read the club notebook?" Kristy asked. We all groaned.

"I thought you promised not to ask us that anymore," said Claud. "I thought you were going to have some *trust* in your best friends!"

The club notebook is kind of like a diary of the jobs we've been on. We're all supposed to write in it after every job and read it once a week or so. It's not really a bad idea — often it's pretty interesting to read and lots of times there's information in it that's helpful to us. But there's something about that notebook. . . . Sometimes it's almost like homework — and Kristy's the teacher.

Anyway, we all said we'd read it. It's a habit by now.

"M&M's?" offered Claud, passing them around. Everyone except for Dawn and me shook out a few. I'm really glad Dawn's a health-food freak because then I'm not the only one always turning down Claud's treats.

"Oh, sorry, Stace — sorry, Dawn. Here, let me find . . ." Claud rummaged around in a box under her bed marked CHARCAOLS. (I told you she hates to study. She's an awful speller.) She came up with a box of whole wheat crackers and tossed it to me. I caught it but handed it right over to Dawn without even opening it. Dawn gave me a curious look, which I pretended not to notice. I didn't really want to call any attention to the fact that my diabetes seemed harder than ever to control.

"Ahem," said Kristy. "Are we all settled? May we proceed with the business at hand?"

Where'd she learn to talk like *that?* We all looked at each other and started to giggle. Kristy looked a little ticked off at first, but then she cracked up, too.

Just then, the phone rang. The first call! Kristy grabbed the phone. "Baby-sitters Club. Can I help you?" She listened for a moment.

"No problem, Mrs. Newton. We'll get right back to you." Kristy hung up and turned to Mary Anne. "How does the schedule look for tomorrow afternoon?" she asked. "Mrs. Newton needs someone to watch Jamie while she takes Lucy to the pediatrician for a checkup."

I'd have liked the job — Jamie's a great kid, and we all like to sit for him — but Mary Anne looked in the record book and reminded me that I already had a job, sitting at the Pikes' with Mallory. (The Pikes are always a two-sitter job.)

"And Jessi has ballet, and Dawn is staying late at school tomorrow, and Claud, you have art class. That leaves you and me, Kristy," Mary Anne continued. She's incredible, the way she keeps the record book up-to-date with all of our activities. Not only that, she's also on top of all the other stuff in the record book, like our rates and customers' addresses and phone numbers. She even has a list of the names of all their pets.

"You take it, Mary Anne. I promised I'd help David Michael give Shannon a bath." Kristy went ahead and called Mrs. Newton to let her know Mary Anne would be there. That's generally the way our club works. We rarely squabble over jobs, because there's always enough to go around.

"Don't forget your Kid-Kit, Mary Anne. I hear it's supposed to rain, and you know how Jamie can be when he's stuck inside," Dawn said.

Kid-Kits are another of Kristy's great ideas. They've been lifesavers more times than I can count, especially on rainy days or when kids miss their parents and need to be distracted. Kid-Kits are boxes filled with toys, books, and games. (We each made our own, decorating them with scraps of cloth, sequins, or whatever else we could find in Claudia's MISSELANIUS carton of supplies. The Kid-Kits don't have all *new* stuff, but it's new to the kids we sit for, and it really keeps them occupied.)

"Speaking of Kid-Kits, how's the treasury? Can we afford some new Colorforms? Mine don't stick anymore, they've been used so much." Kristy looked over at me.

I checked the manila envelope to see how much dues money we had. We each get to keep all the money we earn on every job, but we pay dues weekly to cover incidentals for the Kid-Kits. We also use money from the treasury to pay Kristy's big brother Charlie to drive her to meetings — it's too far to walk since she moved to Watson's — and for the occasional pizza bash, and to help Claud pay her phone bill. It only took me a second to count the money (that's why I'm treasurer).

"There's plenty for Colorforms," I said when I was done. "Anyone else need supplies?"

Everybody started to talk at once, but the phone began to ring. There were four or five calls in a row, but we handled each one quickly. Then, just as Kristy was getting ready to adjourn the meeting, the phone rang one more time.

Kristy answered it. She talked forever. I could tell she was talking to Dr. Johanssen, who is the mother of my favorite baby-sitting charge, Charlotte. But I couldn't figure out what Dr. Johanssen wanted. It sounded complicated.

When she hung up, Kristy pushed back her visor. "Okay, guys, here's the story. Mr. Johanssen's father has to have surgery, and the Johanssens want to be there with him. Dr. Johanssen said her father-in-law isn't in any real danger — but he's pretty old, so the operation could be hard on him. So they have to leave town for about a week, but they don't want to make Charlotte miss school."

I couldn't imagine how they could avoid that. It's not as if Charlotte's other grandparents live here in town. In fact, the Johanssens have no family at all in Stoneybrook.

"So she was wondering if Charlotte could stay with either Jessi's family or with you, Stace," Kristy finished. "She said she's willing to pay well for all the time they'd be away."

This was really something new! No BSC member had ever had this kind of job before.

Right away, Jessi said she couldn't do it. "Too bad. Becca would be so thrilled to have her best friend sleep over for a whole week! But we're going to New Jersey this weekend to see my cousins."

"Let me have the phone, Kristy," I said. "I bet my mom will say it's okay for Charlotte to stay with us." Mom is looking for a job right now (she hasn't worked full-time for years, but now that we're on our own she wants a job), and I knew she'd be glad to watch Charlotte any time I couldn't. Sure enough, she said it was fine, as long as she could have a talk with the Johanssens first.

I called Dr. Johanssen back and told her the good news. She said she'd call my mom right away. I was so excited. I couldn't believe it! I've always wanted a little brother or sister, and having Charlotte around for an entire week would be so much fun. I started to think about all the things we'd do. Where would she sleep? I thought of the guest bedroom, and how nicely I could fix it up for her. I'd use those special sheets Mom had found at a garage sale, and —

"Meeting adjourned," Kristy said. It was six o'clock. I left Claud's house without really even saying good-bye to everyone and biked home. My head was full of plans.

CHAPTER 4

By Thursday, I'd gotten the guest room all
fixed up. I'd made the bed with these great
Raggedy Ann sheets my mom had found. I
knew Charlotte would love them. My old
teddy bear, Goobaw, leaned against the pillow. He was missing one eye and most of his
fur was rubbed bare, but he'd always been a
comfort to me. I had filled a shelf with some
other old dolls and toys that I thought an
eight-year-old might like. There were a couple
of books on the bedside table: *Charlotte's Web*
and *The Long Winter*, two of Charlotte's favorites. I'd even picked some flowers and put
them in a little vase on the windowsill.

I stood in the doorway, surveying the room.
It looked great. I was sure Charlotte would
feel right at home. I walked over to smooth
the sheets one more time, but just then I heard
a car honking in the driveway. I ran to the
window and looked out. It was the Johans-

sens! I ran downstairs and out the door. My mom came out behind me.

Charlotte was struggling to get out of the backseat, which was piled high with suitcases and shopping bags. A suit of Mr. Johanssen's was hanging on one side of the car, and several of Dr. Johanssen's blouses were on the other. Finally Charlotte landed in the driveway. She was clutching a loaded shopping bag and a pillow. Her father pulled a small suitcase out of the space between the front and back seats.

"Is that everything, honey?" he asked.

Charlotte was looking down at the ground. She nodded without saying anything. Suddenly I realized that she was about to cry. I think my mom noticed, too.

"Charlotte, we're so happy to have you visit," she said. "Stacey tells me that spaghetti and meatballs is your favorite supper, and guess what? That's what we're having tonight."

Charlotte managed a tiny smile. I put my arm around her. "What did you bring, Char? Is this shopping bag full of your special stuff?" I asked.

She drew back from me and ran to her father's side. She grabbed him around the waist, and the tears began. "Daddy, please don't go!

I'm going to be so lonely," she cried.

I was surprised, and even though I knew I shouldn't take it personally, I was a little hurt. This was the *old* Charlotte, the shy, clingy girl she'd been when we first met. But she'd come so far since then. The Charlotte I knew now was confident, talkative, and friendly. She was independent, too — after all, she'd been separated from her parents for two whole weeks when we'd all gone off to Camp Mohawk.

Also, I don't mean to sound conceited, but Charlotte really loves me. I've always been her favorite sitter, but it's even more than that. I think she thinks of me as kind of a big sister. She was heartbroken when I moved away from Stoneybrook and thrilled when I came back.

I guess Dr. Johanssen noticed that I was looking a little crestfallen. She took me aside and told me not to feel too bad.

"Charlotte's having an especially hard time with this separation, Stacey. She's really worried about her grandfather — she loves him so much. And even though we've told her that he's going to be fine, she's still afraid. I think she'll be okay once she settles in with you. We are *so* grateful that she can stay here where we'll know she's safe," she said.

Then she walked over to give Charlotte a

hug. Charlotte *really* started crying then, but after both her parents had held her and said their good-byes, they had to leave. I held her hand as they pulled out of the driveway, and we waved until the car was out of sight. As we walked into the house and up the stairs, carrying all the stuff she'd brought, her sobs died down into sniffles interspersed with hiccuppy sighs.

When I opened the door of the guest room, Charlotte really stopped crying for the first time since she'd gotten out of the car.

"Oh, Stacey, this is so neat!" she said. She walked around the room, and I could tell that she was noticing all the little things I'd done to make her feel at home. Charlotte's a pretty thoughtful kid herself, so I knew she'd appreciate my efforts.

She sat on the bed and picked up Goobaw. "My grandpa's very sick," she told him. "He might die."

"Oh, Charlotte, he's not going to die," I said. "He's going to be just fine. And having your parents there with him will help him get better even faster."

I sat next to her on the bed, and this time when I put my arms around her she hugged me right back. "I'm scared, Stacey," she said.

"Of course you are. But everything will be

all right, and we'll have lots of fun while you're here. Tell you what: How about a game of Clue before dinner?" I asked. "You can be Miss Scarlet."

We played and talked until Mom called to us that dinner was ready. By then I thought Charlotte had begun to feel at home. She still sniffed once in awhile, and she kept asking questions about her grandpa's operation ("Does it hurt him when they cut him open?" "But if he's asleep, what if he has a bad dream?"), but she seemed much calmer. (Obviously, Dr. Johanssen hadn't had time to explain the details of the operation to her.)

The spaghetti sauce smelled absolutely delicious. Mom was giving it one last stir as we walked into the kitchen.

"Charlotte, you can sit here, across from Stacey," she said. She filled our plates and brought them to the table. It's usually my job to set the table, but I guess I'd gotten a break on account of Charlotte being there. Then Mom brought her own plate over, along with a huge salad.

We all dug in. All but Charlotte, that is. She just sat there, looking down at her plate as if she didn't recognize what was on it. I knew something had to be wrong, since she usually loves spaghetti.

"What's the matter, Charlotte?" I asked. "Do you want me to cut up your meatballs?" Maybe she just needed a little babying.

"I guess I'm just not hungry," she said in a small voice. "It looks delicious, Mrs. McGill, but . . ." She looked like she was going to cry again.

"That's all right, Charlotte," my mom said. "If you get hungry later there'll be plenty left over." Mom must have been thinking the same thing I was: Charlotte was just feeling too nervous and upset to eat right now. There was no point in forcing her.

I finished my meal quickly while Charlotte waited. I'd told her she could go into the living room and watch TV, but she didn't seem to want to leave my side. She helped me clear the table, and she stuck right by me as I stacked the dishes into the dishwasher.

"Are my parents still on the plane?" she asked. I worked on figuring out the answer. Let's see, I thought. They left for the airport at around 4:30, their flight left at 5:30 and lasted . . . how many hours? But before I could finish my calculations, Charlotte came up with more questions.

"When they land at the airport, what will they do with all those suitcases? Will somebody meet them? Are they going straight to the hospital to see Grandpa?"

I could see that Charlotte needed some distraction. I turned on the TV. Luckily, *The Cosby Show*, one of Charlotte's favorites, was on. That kept her occupied for half an hour, but as soon as it was over, the questions started up again.

"They must be at the hospital by now. Do you think Grandpa is happy to see them? Grandpa must be scared about his operation. How do they close him up again when it's all over?"

Brother. After I'd explained how stitches work and why a zipper wouldn't be practical, I suggested another game of Clue. But halfway through the game I could see that Charlotte was getting restless. How could I distract her before she came up with another round of questions?

"Have you ever played War, Charlotte?" I asked as I dug into my desk drawer for a deck of cards. She had never played that game, so I taught her how. "See, you split the deck in half, and then we each turn over a card at the same time. Whoever has the higher card wins. And when we both turn over the same card, we have a War, like this: one, two, three,

WAR! The winner of that gets all those cards. And whoever gets all the cards in the deck first, wins."

Charlotte loved playing War. Personally, I've always thought it was about the most boring card game on the face of the earth, but that night I played twelve games in a row, very happily. Anything to keep Charlotte's mind off her traveling parents, her sick grandpa, and her own homesickness.

After the twelfth game (which Charlotte won), I suggested that it was time for bed. I had some homework to do once she was asleep, and it was getting late. *Slowly*, she changed into her pajamas. *Slowly* she brushed her teeth. I could see that she was stalling. She was probably nervous about sleeping in a strange bed.

I tucked her in and gave her Goobaw to hold. And then, even though Charlotte is a great reader, I read to her from *Charlotte's Web*. She loves that book, and I love to read to her. "I'm proud to have the same name as *that* spider," she always says.

After three chapters, just as my throat was beginning to hurt from so much reading aloud, I could see that Charlotte's eyelids were drooping. A few moments later, I stopped reading, and sure enough, she'd fallen asleep.

I tiptoed out of the room, leaving the door open a crack so I'd hear her if she woke up. For a moment I thought about skipping my math homework. I was exhausted! I never would have guessed that having Charlotte visit would take so much energy. It would probably get easier as the week went on, I thought. I hoped. I sat down at my desk and blitzed through the math problems as fast as I could.

By the time I finally got into bed I was too tired even to finish a chapter of the book I was reading, *Summer of My German Soldier*. I turned off my light and fell asleep right away. When I woke up the next morning, sunlight was streaming through the window. Birds were singing outside. Mom was puttering around in the kitchen downstairs. And Charlotte was sleeping, all cuddled up next to me in my bed, still clutching Goobaw.

CHAPTER 5

Charlotte and I got home from school at around the same time on Friday. Mom rushed out for a job interview just as I walked in the door. "Hi, girls! See you at dinnertime," she said as she ran out the door. She looked pretty professional, all dressed up in a suit.

I made a snack for the two of us (Triscuits with mustard spread on them and a piece of cheddar cheese on top — yum!), but Charlotte only picked at the food.

"I don't feel so good, Stacey. My throat's all itchy and I feel dizzy," she said.

I felt her forehead, but she didn't seem hot. I thought she was probably just still having a hard time adjusting. After all, she'd made it through a full day of school — how sick could she be? Anyway, she'd survived the first twenty-four hours without her parents, and I knew it could only get easier as time went on. But I figured she could still use some distraction, and I wasn't about to play any more games of War for awhile.

"Let's walk down the street and take a look at that old house they're tearing down," I said. Charlotte agreed to the plan, but first we cleaned up from our snack and changed out of our school clothes. (This all took some time, since Charlotte was still sticking to me like glue.) Finally we set off down the street. I still wasn't all that interested in the old house, but it was something different to do.

It was only about four o'clock when we got to the house, but the workmen had already left for the day. The big old place stood there silently, looking a little forlorn with its porch railings ripped off and its front door gone. There were straggly bushes on both sides of the house and overgrown gardens in front of it. Vines climbed up the porch and twined themselves around the second-story windows. The grass in the yard was almost up to Charlotte's knees. The place seemed oddly quiet all of a sudden.

"Without that front door, the house looks like a person with a tooth missing," said Charlotte. "Let's go inside and look around!"

"No way," I said. "They've started tearing out all the fixtures inside. There could be holes in the floor, or the ceiling might start to come down. We could really get hurt."

My mom had told me that the Stoneybrook Historical Society had asked the developer to save certain parts of the house, since he was being allowed to tear it down. There was supposedly a huge marble fireplace that was in perfect shape, and the society wanted to preserve it. I wondered if they'd taken that out yet. Also, there were supposed to be some neat old lighting fixtures, from way back when Stoneybrook first got electricity. It was going to take awhile to get all that stuff out of the house. Once they'd removed it all, they could just knock down whatever was left.

Charlotte and I walked around the outside of the house, fighting our way through the weeds and brambles. I had to admit that it was a pretty neat old place, even if I didn't think it rated right up there with Gary Rockman as hot news. It was built on a huge scale. There was a long porch that wrapped around the front of it, and a smaller one at the back door. One of the upstairs rooms had big windowed doors that opened out onto a little balcony.

It also had several little towers sticking up here and there. Imagine having your bedroom in one of those round turrets — you could pretend you were Rapunzel or something. Charlotte liked that idea. "Or what if there was a secret trapdoor, so you could be up there and nobody would ever know," she said. One of the things I love about her is her imagination. She is so creative.

As I was checking out the towers, trying to decide which one I would choose for my room, I saw something that made the hair stand up on the back of my neck. There was a face in the window of one of the towers, and it was looking right back at me! I gasped and turned to Charlotte to see if she'd seen it, but she was examining the gingerbread trim on the porch roof. I looked back quickly, but the face had disappeared from the window. Maybe it hadn't really been there in the first place. I was probably just imagining things.

I walked on ahead to catch up with Charlotte. When I found her, her face was dead white. "Did you hear that noise, Stacey?" she asked.

"What noise? I don't hear — " Just then, I *did* hear it. Something was clanking rhythmically. It sounded like chains being dragged across the floors.

"Oh, that's just, um . . . loose pipes! Yeah, that's it. I'm sure it's just the plumbing, Charlotte."

I wasn't really all that sure, but I hoped there

was no way that Charlotte would be able to tell. Anyway, I knew the workmen were also removing some of the plumbing and fixtures for preservation. Mom had said that there were antique radiators and also some of those big old bathtubs that sit on clawed feet. Maybe the men had been working on pulling that stuff out today, and some of the pipes had been left to bang against each other. That really could explain the noises we'd heard. Couldn't it?

We kept walking around the house. It was kind of sad to see it looking so shabby. Most of the windows were broken, and the shutters hung crookedly. The paint was peeling. And what was that near the back door?

I couldn't believe my eyes. It was a gigantic, and I mean *huge*, swarm of gross flies, just like in *The Amityville Horror*. That movie has to be the scariest thing I've ever seen. It's about this family that moves into a house that has ghosts or spirits in it, and all these horrible things keep happening. The flies were the least of it, believe me! Scenes from the movie flashed through my mind as Charlotte and I looked at the flies, but I gritted my teeth, took Charlotte's hand, and kept walking around the house. We'd gone almost all the way around it by now anyway. I wasn't going to let some dumb old spooky house get the better of me.

"Oooooohhhhhhhh . . ."

What was *that?* I looked at Charlotte. Had she moaned? She looked back at me. We kept walking.

"Oooooooooohhhhhhhhh . . ." I heard it again, and this time I knew it hadn't come from Charlotte. It had come from the house. I tightened my grip on her hand, and we took off. That spooky old house *had* gotten the better of me. We were history.

We made it back to my house in record time. Charlotte was looking a little shaky. I was feeling a little shaky myself. But once we were away from the house I felt better. It was like there was a bad feeling coming from that place. I didn't plan to go back there any time soon.

"What do you think made that noise, Stacey? That was scary," said Charlotte.

I couldn't really come up with an answer, and I just wanted to forget all about the house for now, so I dodged the question. "I don't know, Charlotte. But guess what? I have a Baby-sitters Club meeting at five-thirty, and you get to come with me!"

I'd checked with the other members to see if it would be okay to bring Charlotte. With my mom out on a job interview, I didn't know what else to do with her. But even Kristy had said it would be fine to bring her.

Charlotte got all excited. She knew it was an honor to be invited to a club meeting. Not too many "outsiders" had attended meetings. She decided she wanted to change back into her school clothes. This was an important occasion for her.

"Does this mean I'm an honorary member, Stacey?" she asked. "I've always wanted to be in a club, and the Baby-sitters Club is the greatest. Should I bring my allowance money so that I can pay dues?"

I explained that paying dues really wouldn't be necessary, and she looked a little disappointed. To cheer her up, I asked her to help me organize my Kid-Kit. By the time we'd finished that job, it was 5:15. Time to head over to Claudia's. Charlotte begged to be allowed to carry the Kid-Kit, and even though we don't usually bring them to meetings, I said she could.

When we walked into Claud's room, I could feel Charlotte getting shy again. Everybody else was already there, and I guess she felt a little overwhelmed at seeing all the baby-sitters in one place. But then Dawn patted the bed and invited Charlotte to sit next to her.

"Doritos, Charlotte?" Claudia offered the

bag to her. Charlotte just started at Claud's earrings. They *were* pretty wild. One was shaped like a little record, and the other looked like a stereo. I nudged Charlotte.

"Oh! Yes . . . I mean, thanks, Claudia. I love Doritos."

"I like your blouse, Charlotte," said Mary Anne. That was nice of her. Charlotte's blouse wasn't anything special. But Mary Anne is sensitive, and she knew her comment would help put Charlotte at ease.

Kristy took off her visor, leaned over from her spot in the director's chair, and stuck it on Charlotte's head. Charlotte grinned.

"Wait'll we tell you guys what happened this afternoon," I said. "Remember that old house they're tearing down? Well, we went over to take a look at it, and — "

"We heard the scariest noises!" finished Charlotte.

"And you wouldn't believe what I saw," I said.

"Stacey, Charlotte — we want to hear all about it, but it's time to start the meeting," said Kristy. She brought the meeting to order, and we took care of business for awhile. The phone rang a few times and we assigned jobs. Then there was a lull in the action.

"Claud, remember that movie we saw, *The*

Amityville Horror? Well, this afternoon was just like a scene out of that movie, I swear," I said. "Remember those flies?"

Claudia shrieked. "Ew! I'll never forget them. They were totally disgusting."

"Well, we saw a whole swarm of them over at that house. And I saw a face at one of the windows, too."

Charlotte looked at me. I hadn't told her about that. I'd figured she was scared enough as it was.

"It was probably just one of the workmen," said Dawn.

"Yeah," said Jessi. "He was probably surprised to see you, too."

"No, that was the really weird thing," I said. "There were no workmen. They were all gone — long gone, it looked like. And it was only around four when we got there, too."

Charlotte looked really scared all over again. In fact, she looked like she might start crying. Kristy must have noticed, too, because just then the phone rang and she said, "Charlotte, want to answer that?"

Charlotte looked over at Kristy. "Me?" she asked.

"Yeah, you!" said Kristy.

Charlotte beamed. Then she realized she'd

better grab the phone. It'd been ringing for awhile by then.

"Baby-Sitters Club," she said. "No job too small!"

The room was quiet for half a second as we all looked at each other. Mallory was the first to crack up, and soon we were all hysterical. Charlotte was a natural!

CHAPTER 6

Saturday

You guys would not believe the sitting experience I had on Friday. Mom and Watson had tickets to something or other, Nannie had taken off in the Pink Clinker for League Night at the bowling alley, and Sam and Charlie naturally had plans, so it was just me and the Wild Bunch: Karen and Andrew, David Michael, and of course Emily Michelle. Maybe if we hadn't had a storm that night Karen wouldn't have gotten started on the Ben Brewer stories, and the whole evening would have gone differently... maybe, but somehow I doubt it. First she started in on the Morbidda Destiny stories, though...

"And if she ever catches Boo-Boo again, she's going to put a spell on him. He'll still *look* like Boo-Boo, and he'll still come when we call him, but something about him will be different. He won't purr anymore, and his tongue will be as cold as ice, not warm like it is now." Karen was really on a roll.

Andrew was sitting on Kristy's lap, and David Michael was huddled on the floor near her feet. Emily Michelle was rooting through the toy basket, looking for her "baby." She was the only one in the room who wasn't spellbound by Karen's tale.

Kristy usually has no patience for Karen's silly ghost stories, but after hearing what Charlotte and I had been through that afternoon, she was all set to be totally spooked.

It wasn't that late yet, but the sky was completely dark. Thunder rumbled in the distance, and lightning flickered. The storm was on its way.

Andrew looked up at Kristy. "She won't really do that, will she? I like Boo-Boo the way he is."

Kristy shook herself. Andrew really looked scared. She had to break the mood before things got out of hand. "Of course not, Andrew. Karen's just telling stories again. Listen, you guys. How about if I make a big bowl of popcorn and we play a game or two of Chutes and Ladders?"

"Popcorn! Yea!" said David Michael. "Can we play the Name Game while you make it?"

Kristy sighed. The Name Game gets tiresome fast, but the kids love it. "Okay. Who's first?"

"Me!"

"I am!"

"No, me!"

They all yelled at once. Kristy should have known better. She stalled for time, opening and closing cupboards and setting up the popper. "Okay, let's do Emily first. Then *she* can decide who's next. Ready? Here goes." And Kristy started to sing:

> *"Emily Emily bo bemily*
> *Bananafana fo femily*
> *Me mi mo memily*
> *Emily!"*

Karen joined in, and so did David Michael. Andrew got some of the words right, but he got stuck on the "bananafana" part and just kept doing it over and over.

"Who's next, Emily?" Kristy asked. Emily pointed to Karen, who's a favorite of hers. They all sang, Karen loudest of all.

> *"Karen Karen bo baren*
> *Bananafana fo faren*
> *Me mi mo maren*
> *Karen!"*

The Name Game continued as Kristy made the popcorn. Running out of names didn't stop them: They just went around the kitchen, singing about everything they saw:

> *"Toaster toaster bo boaster*
> *Bananafana fo foaster*
> *Me mi mo moaster*
> *Toaster!"*

Things got pretty silly for awhile. When the popcorn was done they trooped into the living room to play Chutes and Ladders. The game wasn't half over when Karen started up again.

"I heard Ben Brewer walking around last night. His footsteps went up and down, up and down. He was pacing. He was restless. Finally he stopped and sat down. I heard the bed creak. Then he took off his boots. The first one dropped. *Boom*. Then the second."

And just as she said "second," there was a huge clap of thunder. Everybody jumped, and Karen shrieked and leapt into Kristy's lap. She'd even scared *herself* that time. Her Ben Brewer stories are about the ghost who supposedly lives on the third floor. (Proof? Boo-Boo won't go above the second floor. Animals are sensitive to ghostly presences, according to Karen.) Karen's stories are mostly old hat by now. But the storm's timing had sure contributed to the drama of this one.

Thunder was really booming then, and the yard outside was lit up by lightning. It was pouring. Kristy had all four kids piled into her lap, and they just sat and hugged each other and watched the storm. Finally the thunder and lightning moved on, though the wind and rain didn't seem to let up much.

"Okay, time for bed, you guys," Kristy said. "David Michael, Andrew, and Karen, brush your teeth and get your pajamas on. I'll put Emily Michelle down and then come and read to all of you."

Kristy knew that the kids were a little spooked, but it had gotten late while they waited for the storm to pass, so she figured they'd be sleepy.

No such luck. She read five chapters of *Ozma of Oz* (they were going through all the Oz books, since they'd just seen the movie), and everyone was still wide awake. Then she sang some lullabies with them. "All the Pretty Little Ponies" was Karen's favorite. The Ghostbusters song, "Who Ya Gonna Call" was David Michael's. Finally Kristy tucked them all in, sleepy or not, and told them it was bedtime. She went downstairs and sat on the couch to read.

"Kristee-e-e-e-e, I need a drink of wa-a-a-a-ter." That was David Michael. He was in a whiny mood. Kristy brought the water, and he made her stay while he drank it. She waited, then closed the door to his room almost all the way and went back downstairs.

"Kristy?"

Karen was standing at the door of the living room. "I can hear Ben again," she said. "He's walking around."

"It's just the wind," said Kristy. "Go back to bed, Karen."

Then Emily called, and of course Andrew wanted a drink, too. Kristy thought they'd never go to sleep. But finally the house was quiet. Quiet, that is, except for the wind rattling the shutters outside.

Kristy found that she couldn't concentrate on her book. In fact, she couldn't stop thinking about the old house and the experiences Charlotte and I had there.

She wandered into the kitchen and ate the last handful of popcorn. She washed out the bowl. She opened the refrigerator door, looked inside, and closed it without having any idea of what she'd seen in there. Then she tiptoed upstairs to check on her brothers and sisters. Everybody was fast asleep. Kristy figured that that was a good thing, except that all of a sudden she felt kind of lonely. (I think she was at what my mom would call "loose ends.")

Finally, Kristy ended up downstairs in the library. (That's right. Watson's mansion is so big that there's a whole room just for his books.) The library at Watson's is a cozy place, with big red leather armchairs, lamps that look like they're made out of stained glass, and, of course, hundreds — maybe thousands — of books.

Kristy looked around and spotted a big carton in the corner. She remembered Watson telling her that he'd just bought some old books at an estate sale. She also remembered him saying that some of the books were about the history of Stoneybrook. She was hoping that maybe she could find something out about that old house!

She pulled a couple of books out of the box and took a look at them. They were kind of dusty, and they smelled like they'd been in someone's basement for awhile. The covers were cracked and the edges of the pages were yellowed. She opened one of them. Right away she spotted the name Brewer. Wow! Watson's family really *had* lived in Stoney-brook for a long time.

She kept reading, just standing there by the cardboard box. There were other names she recognized, and places, too. Of course, there was no record of her old neighborhood: That whole area had just been woods and farmland at one time. But she found a chapter on the building of the library, and one on what the great blizzard of '88 had done to Stoneybrook. (That actually sounded kind of fun — people could walk out onto the snow from their second-story windows!)

Kristy took an armload of books over to one of the armchairs. She switched on a lamp, made herself comfortable, and settled in to read. The storm still blew outside, making the doors shake. Rain splattered against the windows. But Kristy was lost in "Olde Stoneybrooke."

She couldn't find a thing about the old house, though. She skimmed through each of the books, looking for information on the turreted mansion. Then she went back and paged through each one again. There was absolutely nothing.

She was about to give up when a crumbly piece of paper fell out of the book she was holding. She unfolded it carefully, but even so, it ripped a little along the crease. It was very, very old. It was a map.

It looked hand-drawn, and the locations were all hand-lettered. She turned it this way and that, trying to figure out how it related to the town she knew. It was a very early map of Stoneybrook. Only a scattering of houses were shown, along with a bank and a church. The church was still there, and so was . . . the house itself. Kristy had finally located "our" old house. At first she couldn't quite make out the writing in the area in and around the house. What did it say?

"Oh, my lord," said Kristy out loud. (That's one of Claud's favorite expressions, and we've all picked it up.)

From what she could see on this incredibly

old map, Kristy figured out that the entire town of Stoneybrook had been built over ancient burial grounds. And "our" house was built on — oh, my lord — the most sacred spot of all!

Kristy noticed that the map was shaking. Then she figured out that it was her hands that were shaking. She let go of the map and it drifted to the floor. Kristy thought again about all the things that Charlotte and I had told her that day. She was scared out of her wits.

She decided not to read another word in those books. She decided to put the map away and never look at it again. She decided she wished that her mom and Watson would come home SOON.

Kristy got up and turned off the lamp she'd been using. She picked up all the books and brought them over to the carton in the corner. As she packed them away, she suddenly got the strangest feeling that she was being watched (she told me this later). There was a definite presence in the room. She didn't want to turn around, so she just kept packing the books into the box, very carefully. The presence was still there. Finally, she knew she had to turn and look. She wheeled around quickly and saw Sam and Charlie just standing there in the doorway, grinning and making horrible faces at her. She screamed and fell into the nearest chair. Sam and Charlie didn't stop laughing for at least half an hour.

CHAPTER 7

I was walking down Fifth Avenue, past Rockefeller Center. Gary Rockman was running after me, calling my name over and over.

"Stacey," he said. "Stacey, please come to me!"

I woke up with a start, back in my regular old bed in Stoneybrook. It was morning. Gary Rockman was nowhere in sight, but someone *was* calling my name. It was Charlotte, and she didn't sound too good.

I went into the guest room. Charlotte was in bed, the covers tangled around her legs. She looked flushed and hot. I put my hand on her forehead. She was burning up!

"Stacey, my throat hurts. I feel awful." Charlotte *looked* awful. A couple of tears ran down her cheeks. "I miss my mommy," she said.

"I know, Charlotte, but don't worry. We'll

take good care of you." I ran for the thermometer, and while Charlotte held it in her mouth, I went to find my mom. She came upstairs with me and we took a look at the thermometer. A hundred and two degrees. Charlotte was definitely sick. Mom and I glanced at each other. I knew she was feeling as bad as I was for the way we'd played down Charlotte's earlier symptoms. I'd been so sure it was just that Charlotte was nervous and homesick.

Charlotte's parents had left a list of emergency numbers. I checked it to see which doctor we should call, and it said she went to Dr. Dellenkamp. Mom went downstairs to call for an appointment. I helped Charlotte get up, wash her face, and get dressed. She moved slowly. Finally we all piled into the car and drove to the doctor's office.

When we walked into the waiting room, we could see right away that it was going to be awhile before we saw the doctor. There was a woman with a crying baby, another mother trying to convince her toddler to sit and play quietly with some blocks, and a girl about my age who was sitting there alone, kind of hunched over. She looked like she had a stomachache. Mom decided that she might as well get the grocery shopping done, since I was there to wait with Charlotte, so she took off.

Charlotte and I sat down on the couch. It was kind of an ugly couch, made of that fake leather stuff that sticks to your legs when you try to get up. Why do waiting rooms always have such ugly furniture? Charlotte put her head in my lap and closed her eyes. I stroked her hair. It's the worst feeling when you're sick and you have to be anywhere but home in bed.

Charlotte seemed comfortable, so I looked at the table by the couch to see what magazines they had. Oh, boy. I had a choice between a July 1979 *Reader's Digest* and this month's *Highlights for Children*. I picked up *Highlights*, just to see if it had changed any since I used to look at it in *my* pediatrician's office. Nope. There were good old Goofus and Gallant, same as ever. Even as a kid I'd thought that Gallant was kind of a goody-goody.

I was still paging through the magazine when the outer door opened and the most gorgeous guy walked in, holding the hand of a little boy who must have been his brother. I stared. Blond curly hair, blue eyes . . . he reminded me of Scott, this lifeguard I'd had a crush on once in Sea City, New Jersey. He looked back at me, and then I saw his gaze fall to the magazine I was holding. I dropped it like a hot potato. He smiled at me, as if to say he understood.

I was totally humiliated. Luckily, the receptionist called Charlotte then, and I went with her into the examining room, still blushing.

The examination didn't take long. Dr. Dellenkamp knew what it was right away.

"Tonsillitis *again?*" Charlotte wailed.

"That's right, Charlotte. Back on the old penicillin," the doctor said. "We may have to do something about those tonsils at some point," she said to me quietly as Charlotte hopped off the table. "But for now, since her parents are away, we'll just hit the germs again with this." She wrote out a prescription.

"Charlotte has trouble taking pills, so we usually give her liquid penicillin. She should take a teaspoon of it four times a day. She'll feel better pretty quickly — in a day or so, I'd say."

The doctor put her arm around Charlotte as we walked out. "I know you must miss your parents, but you be a good patient for Stacey. She'll take care of you just fine," she said. She winked at me as we said good-bye.

My mom was waiting for us. Fortunately, the gorgeous guy was busy keeping his little brother's hands out of the aquarium, so I was able to dash out of the waiting room without meeting his eyes again.

We stopped by the drugstore to pick up Charlotte's prescription. As soon as she saw the bottle she started to . . . well, she started to whine. There's no nicer way to put it.

"I *hate* that stuff," she moaned. "It tastes so awful that I want to throw up when I take it. Do I have to take it? Oh, I want my mommy. It's not fair!"

I knew how she felt, but really. Her whining was a little hard to take, especially since she didn't let up the whole way home.

When we got to our house, I went into the kitchen for a spoon. Charlotte stayed in the living room, where she'd thrown herself on the couch. When I walked in, she turned over so that her face was buried in the pillows.

"I *won't* take it," she said. "I'd rather be sick."

I rolled my eyes. "Charlotte, look. It says 'New Cherry Flavor' on the bottle. Maybe it'll taste better than last time." I opened the bottle and sniffed the liquid inside. Oh, ew. It *did* smell vile. There's nothing worse than that fake "cherry" flavor, unless it's phony banana. Yick.

"It smells okay, Charlotte," I lied. "Come on, all you have to take is a teaspoon. If you hold your nose, you'll hardly taste it. And I'll make you an ice-cream soda with ginger ale. You can drink that to take away the bad taste." I was bribing her, and I knew it. This wasn't the right way to go about getting that medicine down her throat.

"No," she said flatly. Oh, well. My bribe hadn't worked anyway. She burrowed deeper into the couch cushions. This was really getting frustrating. I tried not to feel angry at Charlotte. She wasn't feeling well, she missed her parents, she was worried about her grandpa, and she was stuck in a strange house. I guess I might have felt cranky and uncooperative, too, if I'd been her.

If I were her. . . . Suddenly I had a brainstorm. Maybe taking just a teaspoon full of nasty medicine wouldn't seem all that terrible if she could see what I had to go through every day, just to stay healthy. It just might work.

"Charlotte, you know I have diabetes, right?" I knew she knew, because I've discussed my diabetes with Dr. Johanssen, in front of Charlotte.

Charlotte kind of grunted, but she didn't budge from her "nest" in the couch.

"Want me to show you the medicine I have to take?" I asked. "We'll forget about yours for now."

That got her moving. She followed me upstairs and I opened the desk drawer where I keep all my equipment. I tried to explain a little bit about diabetes and why it makes me sick and how insulin helps to keep it in check. I'm not sure how well she followed me. She'd probably never heard of a "pancreas" before.

"I didn't used to have to do this, but since I haven't been feeling too well lately, now I have to check my glucose level a few times a day," I said. "All I do is prick my finger, like this — "

Charlotte gasped as I pricked my finger and squeezed out a tiny drop of blood. I wiped it onto something called a test strip and put the strip into a little machine. In a minute the number came up. 110. That was just about normal for me at this time of day. Charlotte was fascinated.

"Knowing what my number is helps me

make sure to take the right amount of insulin. When I'm ready to take my insulin, I load up this syringe and give myself a shot." I wasn't going to show her how I did that. It might really scare her.

The shots don't hurt me anymore — I'm so used to them by now. But to someone else, especially someone Charlotte's age, it might be frightening.

I told her some more about what it meant to be a diabetic. Like how this was something I'd have to deal with every day for the rest of my life. And how I had to be extremely careful about what I ate, and why. Charlotte's eyes got rounder and rounder. She'd had no idea of what I went through just to control my illness.

"Shots every single day? Oh, Stacey, you're so brave," she said when I'd finished explaining everything.

"Not really, Charlotte. This is just how things are for me. I don't have any choice in the matter," I said. "Anyway, it feels good to take care of myself."

Well, after all that, it was no trick at all to get Charlotte to take her medicine. She barely made a face as she swallowed it down.

"Good girl," I said. "Now, let's get you into bed."

She changed into her pajamas while I put a clean pillowcase on her pillow. I always think it feels good to have a fresh pillowcase to rest your head on when you're sick. I also set up her room for the day. I brought in our little portable TV and stocked the shelves with more games, drawing paper and crayons, and books.

While Charlotte got settled into bed, I went down to the kitchen to make her a snack. I set up a tray with that ice-cream soda I'd promised her. When I'm sick, my mom always puts a flower in a little vase on my dinner tray, so I did that, too. Charlotte deserved to be spoiled a little; just think, she'd been getting sick all that time and nobody had paid attention to her complaints. I got myself a glass of ice water and took the tray upstairs.

Charlotte and I spent the whole day in her room, playing every game I had. Yes, that does include War, if you're wondering. We also watched TV and I read to her for awhile before she dropped off for a nap. While she slept, I just stayed in the room and read to myself. It was a peaceful afternoon.

That night, Charlotte called her parents. She wanted to let them know that she was sick but getting better. She also wanted to check on her grandfather. She talked to her mom for just a few minutes, and by the end of the call she was beaming. Her grandpa's operation had gone very well and he was feeling much better. The Johanssens would be back home on Thursday, just as they'd planned. Charlotte was definitely on the road to recovery.

CHAPTER 8

By Sunday morning, Charlotte was feeling much better. Penicillin does work fast. It hadn't been easy getting her to take her medicine on schedule — she still hated it — but at least she had taken most of it.

Charlotte came downstairs for breakfast, and Mom made special sugar-free blueberry pancakes. Yum. I love them because they're so good on their own that I don't even miss being able to have maple syrup. Charlotte ate a big stack of them. She was definitely better.

But Dr. Dellenkamp had said that even if she was feeling all right, Charlotte should take it easy on Sunday and Monday. She wasn't supposed to go to school until Tuesday.

Tuesday seemed a long way off. I was sick of playing War, sick of being Professor Plum in Clue, and very sick of TV. I was even sick of reading *Charlotte's Web*.

What were we going to do all day? I think

Charlotte was just as tired as I was of being cooped up, especially now that she was feeling more normal.

Then I remembered that Kristy had called on Saturday to tell me about some map she'd found on Friday night. Maybe she could come over and bring the map, along with some of those old books of Watson's. Kristy had said she really hadn't found much in the books, but maybe if we went through them all, we'd come up with something. It would be fun to play detective, anyway. I called Kristy up.

"Kristy, it's Stace. What're you doing today?"

"I've got no plans," she said. "I don't even have to watch the kids, since Mom and Watson took them to the mall to shop for shoes."

"How about bringing over that old map and the books?" I said. "Charlotte's home sick, here, and we'd love to look at them."

"Great," said Kristy. "Hold on, let me see if Nannie can drive me over."

The arrangements were made. While we waited for Kristy, Charlotte and I washed the breakfast dishes. Then she took her medicine without fussing too much. Finally we settled in on the front steps (Charlotte had felt good enough to get dressed that morning) and waited for Kristy to show up. While we waited, we talked about the old house.

"I'm glad we were together when we heard those noises, Stacey," said Charlotte. "That was scary. But you know, I feel like there's something interesting about that house. I hope we can find out more about it."

I told her a little about the map Kristy had found, but not too much. I thought that the idea of burial grounds might be a little too much for Charlotte, but she seemed fascinated.

By the time Kristy got out of the Pink Clinker (Nannie's old car) in front of our house, Charlotte's excitement was at an all-time high.

"Where are the books, Kristy?" she asked, without even saying hello. She would have dived into the backseat and hauled out the box if I hadn't stopped her.

"Easy, Charlotte. You're still sick, remember?" I said. "I know you love mysteries, but let's take our time. We've got all day."

Charlotte does love mysteries, and I have to say that she's a pretty good sleuth. She played a big part in solving the mystery of an old diary that Mallory had found in a trunk in our attic. That mystery had led us to find the portrait of a beautiful woman, which now hung over our fireplace. Back then, we thought my house might be haunted, but that was nothing compared to what we were facing now.

We brought the box of books inside and spread ourselves out in the living room. We each took a book and began to read. After awhile we traded books and read some more. Kristy had been right. There wasn't much in them. They were interesting, but we couldn't see any clues to the mystery of the old house.

"Where's that map, Kristy?" I asked. "Let's take a look at it."

Kristy took it out and opened it carefully.

"Wow, that's really old, isn't it?" asked Charlotte. "The writing on it is so weird. What does it say?"

I couldn't make it out too well, either, but it did seem to show that house. As far as the burial-ground business, I couldn't be sure. The map wasn't like any I'd ever seen. It had strange signs and symbols on it, and markings in a faded red color. I wondered if it was the real McCoy or just something someone had made up for fun.

"How do we know that this map is really as old as it looks?" I asked.

Kristy and Charlotte both just gave me a look. They wanted to believe in the map and in the mystery of the old house. They had no doubts about the map being genuine.

"I wonder who owns that house," I said. I

was really starting to get interested in that "dumb old house," in spite of myself. Laine would never believe it. If she ever got involved in a mystery back in New York, it would probably have to do with something like, "Who stole the countess's jewels from the hotel safe?" or "Does the ghost of Elvis haunt the Hard Rock Cafe?"

"I don't know who owns it. Nobody's lived there for years," Kristy said. "But I don't remember there ever being a 'for sale' sign in front of that house."

"Do you think the owner is even still alive?" asked Charlotte. She gulped. "Maybe that was his ghost we heard."

"No, he must be alive somewhere. How else could that developer ever have bought the house in order to knock it down?" Kristy looked thoughtful. "I wonder if we could find him."

"You keep saying 'he,' " I said. "The owner *could* be a woman, you know. Anyway, how can we find out who the owner is? Do you think *she* still lives in the area?"

"We could find out everything we need to know about the house if only we could track him — or her — down," said Kristy. "Maybe Mary Anne would have some good ideas. Her family has lived around here for a long time."

I went to the phone and dialed Mary Anne's number. Luckily, she was home.

"Mary Anne, did you hear about the map that Kristy found?" I asked, after we'd said hello, how are you, and all that. She hadn't, so I told her about it.

"It sounds like a mystery, all right," she said. "But where do we go from here?" I didn't know what to tell her.

Kristy motioned for me to give her the phone. "Mary Anne," she said. "Keep on the lookout for clues. You never know where you might find one. Maybe there are some old books or documents somewhere in that old house of yours."

Since Mary Anne lived with Dawn now, they really might find some clues in their house. It's one of the oldest houses around here, and it has some mysteries of its own. That secret passage has been the site of all kinds of strange happenings.

"Dawn's out sitting for the Rodowskys, but as soon as she gets back I'll ask her if she's got any ideas," said Mary Anne. "It's kind of fun to have another mystery to solve, isn't it?"

Next we called Claudia. She got all excited about the books and the map, and she wanted to come right over and look at them and hear more about what Kristy had found out. She was stuck at home, though, doing homework. (Claud's really smart — even if she isn't an actual genius like her sister, Janine — but her grades don't show it. If she doesn't keep her grades up she might have to quit the Baby-sitters Club. No way did we want that to happen.)

"Stay put and do your homework, Claud," I said. "But keep your eyes and ears open in the next few days. You can never tell where or when a clue might turn up."

We tried to call Mallory, since she loves mysteries, too, but Mrs. Pike said that Mal had taken Margo and Claire (two of her little sisters) on a special Teddy Bears' Picnic. Mal's such a terrific big sister. I remembered now that she'd been planning this for awhile. She was going to make little sandwiches and "tea," and help the girls dress up their teddy bears in special outfits. It sounded like fun. I asked Mrs. Pike to tell Mallory to call me back when she got home.

We didn't even try to call Jessi, since we knew she was away for the weekend. So that was everyone. If we all kept on the alert for clues, maybe we could crack this case.

To be honest, I didn't really even know for sure if we had a mystery on our hands. This burial-ground story was hard to prove, and that old map was so hard to read. I wasn't positive that Kristy had gotten it right. Maybe all that stuff we'd seen and heard at the house was just our imaginations. Maybe we were making something out of nothing.

But there was Charlotte, sitting on the couch with one of Watson's old books. She was flipping through it one more time, combing for clues. I could see that, for awhile anyway, she'd forgotten that she was sick. She'd forgotten that she was stuck inside for another day and a half. And she'd forgotten that her parents were a plane ride away. Mystery or not, the old house was keeping us both busy, and I was thankful for that.

CHAPTER 9

monday

    I know you guys dont think of the wordes 'libary' and 'Cloud' as belonging in the same sentense, but boy, they do now. I never knewe just how much you coud find out just by looking in a few reference books. maybe when Im older Ill will be a libarian like my mom oh yeah, P.S. Gabie and miryiah had a grate time at the libary to.

On Monday, Claud had a job sitting for the Perkins girls, Gabbie and Myriah. Gabbie's almost three, and Myriah's almost six. We all like them a lot. They also have a baby sister named Laura. Mrs. Perkins was taking Laura to Dr. Dellenkamp to have her cough checked out.

When Claudia arrived, Chewy — the Perkinses' big black Labrador retriever — was running around in circles. Myriah was holding his favorite toy, a disgusting, ancient well-chewed tennis ball. She wouldn't throw it for him, and it was driving him nuts. He barked as he ran, begging her to throw it.

"Claudee Kishi!" yelled Gabbie. "Hi, Claudee Kishi! Toshe me up!" Gabbie always calls us by our full names, and "toshe me up" is an expression she invented and uses all the time. Basically, it means, "Pick me up and give me a big hug." Claud was glad to oblige, since Gabbie is an extremely huggable girl.

"I have a great idea, guys," said Claud. "How about if we go to the library for Story Hour? Today they're going to read a couple of your favorite books. Guess which ones. *Mike Mulligan and His Steam Shovel* and *The Little House*. And then, after they read the books, everybody gets to help make a mural of the town in *The Little House*."

Claud had found out about Story Hour from her mom. Mrs. Kishi is the head librarian, so she knows about all the stuff that goes on there. Claud had thought she'd check out Story Hour to see if it was a good way to spend some time with the kids we were sitting for.

"Yea!" yelled Gabbie. "What's a mural?"

"It's a big, giant picture, Gabbers," said Myriah. "Can Chewy come, Claudia? Oh, boy, I can't wait!"

They do love those two books. Have you ever read *The Little House*? It's about this house that was once in the country, and then slowly a big city gets built up around it. I won't spoil the ending, but trust me, it's a great book.

Claud had another motive for going to the library. She couldn't stop thinking about the old house being on the site of a burial ground. Maybe, she thought, she could find out more by browsing through the local history section. Claud must have been *obsessed* with that house: It's not like her to do much voluntary reading (besides Nancy Drew, of course).

She piled Gabbie and Myriah into the Perkinses' big red wagon — she'd vetoed the idea of Chewy coming along — and set off for the library. The girls were excited about going, since the library is one of their favorite places. They go every week to check out books and this would be like a bonus visit for them.

"Can we take out a book today, Claudee Kishi?" asked Gabbie.

"I want to take out *five* books," said Myriah. "This many," she added, holding up all five fingers on her right hand. "Because I'm five years old. Five and a half, really. Right, Claudia?"

"That's right, Myriah. And you can both take out as many books as you like today," said Claudia. "Did you know that my mommy is the boss of the whole library?" she added.

"Does she *live* there?" asked Myriah. "I always wanted to sleep overnight at the library. I bet she gets to whenever she wants."

Claudia's mom had told us once that kids really do think she lives at the library. After all, she's always there! When they see her somewhere else in town, like at the supermarket, sometimes they just stop and stare at her. They can't believe she's just like a regular person. She's the "liberrian."

Claud cleared up Myriah's confusion, and the girls settled into the trip.

"The sun'll come out tomorrow," sang Gabbie.

"Bet your bottom dollar there'll be sun," chimed in Myriah.

Claudia smiled as she pulled them along. Gabbie and Myriah seem to know all the words to a million songs, and they love to sing them all the way through. After they finished "Tomorrow," they ran through "You're Never Fully Dressed Without a Smile." They must have seen *Annie* a couple of hundred times.

"I know you, I danced with you once upon a dream," sang Myriah. They'd started to act out their favorite scenes from *Sleeping Beauty*. Myriah was playing the part of the prince.

"Oh! I have to go now!" said Gabbie, dramatically. She was Sleeping Beauty. She was very convincing in the role.

When they got to the library, Claud stopped into the office to see her mom. The girls followed her quietly. They know how to behave in the library, especially when the big boss is looking right at them.

Claudia then settled the girls in the children's room. Story Hour was just about to start. They were right on time. Then she headed back into the main room. She'd forgotten where the local history books were kept, even though we've looked at them before. But there was no way she was going to ask her mom. It was embarrassing to be the head librarian's daughter and not even know her way around the library. Fortunately this guy we know, Bruce Schermerhorn, is working there as a page, shelving the books that people return. Claud asked him where the books were, and he helped her find the ones she wanted.

She took them to a chair where she could be comfortable and also keep an eye on Gabbie and Myriah. They seemed to be having a good time listening to the stories.

The first two volumes Claudia looked at were hard to get through. They were the kind of dry historical books that are absolutely no fun to read. But Claud did her best. It wasn't easy for her, trying to plow through that material. Still, she stuck with it. Finally she realized that she wasn't getting anywhere.

She picked up one of the other books and took a look at it. It seemed to be full of old records of the town of Stoneybrook. There were birth records and death records and property-tax records and even a map. This stuff looked even more boring than what she'd looked at before. Claud gritted her teeth and kept looking. She was determined to get *something* out of this visit to the library.

She picked up a second book of old town

records and worked her way through it until her eyes lit on a couple of paragraphs that looked as though they had something to do with "our" house. From what she'd read so far, it *did* seem as though the town was built on ancient burial grounds. And the house *was*, she thought, on a sacred spot. The people who had written down the records didn't seem to be too concerned about it, but Claud was getting chills up and down her spine. How could anyone think that such a thing didn't matter? What about the spirits of the dead who had been buried there? How could they ever be at rest with houses and banks and Burger Kings on top of them?

Claud got a grip on herself. Before she totally flew off the handle, she knew she should keep looking to see if she could find out who owned the house. Property tax records should be just the ticket, she thought. She kept poring over the musty old book. And then she found it! The owner's name. Ronald Hennessey. It was right there in black and white.

Claud felt like cheering. This was a major discovery. But what good did a name do unless she could find out more about who Ronald Hennessey was? Was he still alive? Where did he live now? He sure didn't live in the house he owned, and he hadn't for years.

Claud sat for a moment and thought. Where could she look next? She glanced into the children's room. All the Story Hour kids were working on a big messy mural full of apartment buildings and highways. There seemed to be dinosaurs roaming the streets, too. The Little House stood forlornly in the middle of the picture. Story Hour was almost over.

Finally, Claud went over to her mom's desk. "Mom, where would you look to see if someone who used to live in Stoneybrook still *does* live in Stoneybrook?"

Mrs. Kishi looked up at Claudia, surprised. She must have wondered what Claud was up to, but she didn't ask. She just smiled a little and said, "Well, I guess I'd try the phone book."

Claudia told me later that she wished there was a trapdoor she could fall into right then. How dumb she'd been! She'd gotten so wrapped up in her complicated historical research that she'd never even thought of using a regular old phone book.

She went to the reference desk, where they keep all the phone books for the whole country. She found the local one and opened it right up to the exact page that Ronald Hennessey was on. Guess what. He was in there. It was as easy as that.

Claud looked at the address listed. Stoney-brook Manor. That was a nursing home. Of course, Mr. Hennessey must be pretty old by now, she realized. She copied down the address and went off to collect Gabbie and Myriah.

Story Hour was just ending, but Claud had to hang around for awhile as the girls picked out some books to take home. Gabbie just kind of grabbed randomly, but Myriah seemed to have definite ideas about which ones she liked and which ones were "ucky." While she waited, Claud strolled over to look at the finished mural. There was a lot going on in that picture, a lot that the illustrator of *The Little House* wouldn't recognize. Besides the dinosaurs, there were soldiers with amazing weaponry, witches holding brooms, ballerinas, and a Candy Land-like area where lollipops grew. It was a great mural.

Finally, the girls had all the books they wanted. They went to the desk to check them out.

"What's your name?" asked the lady at the desk.

"Gabbie," said Gabbie. "What's yours?"

Claudia laughed and went over to help. "These are the Perkins girls," she said. "Gabbie and Myriah." The clerk must have been new, or else she'd have recognized them. She looked up their cards and checked out the books. It had turned out to be a pretty big stack, so Claud helped carry them out to the wagon.

The girls piled in with their books and spent the trip home telling each other and Claudia the story of Mike Mulligan. They decided that Mike should have lived *in* the Little House.

Claud got them home just as Mrs. Perkins returned from the doctor's office. Dr. Dellenkamp had given her a prescription for Laura and said that she'd be fine in no time.

By then it was almost time for the Baby-sitters Club meeting, so Claud ran home as soon as she'd said her good-byes to the girls and to Mrs. Perkins. She was excited about what she'd found out and proud of herself for sticking with the research. She was dying to tell us all about Mr. Ronald Hennessey.

CHAPTER 10

While Claudia was doing her research at the library, Charlotte and I were doing some research of our own.

It was Monday afternoon. I'd gotten home from school to find Charlotte feeling "all well," as she had put it. My mom, who had spent the day with Charlotte, headed out to do some errands.

"There's a snack set out for you on the table, honey," she said. Sometimes she still treats me like a fourth-grader, which isn't such a terrible thing. It's nice to feel taken care of.

I sat down with Charlotte and ate my fruit and crackers while she told me about her day. Since she'd been home all day, her story wasn't that exciting: She'd watched TV, read, and taught my mom how to play War. But it was nice to come home to find my "little sis-ter" waiting for me. I'd really been enjoying Charlotte's company, probably even more than if she really *were* my little sister. Real sisters do things like fight and tease each other, and we never do that. We just have a good time together.

After I'd eaten, Charlotte followed me upstairs. I wanted to change out of my school clothes, since I'd worn a new outfit that day and I wanted to keep it nice. I'd gotten this pink polka-dotted short skirt with suspender straps and had worn it with an oversized white T-shirt. I had on my pink high-top sneakers, folded down to show their striped lining. I'd also worn these great earrings Claud had given me for my last birthday. They had all these little pink plastic hearts dangling down from one bigger heart. In case you haven't noticed, I do like the color pink!

By the time I'd finished changing, Charlotte and I had decided to take a walk. Charlotte was feeling great — she'd be able to go to school the next day, for sure — and she wanted to get outside. Guess where we went. That's right. There was something about that old house. We just couldn't stay away from it.

When we got there, the workmen were packing up their tools and getting ready to leave. It was early again, not even four o'clock yet, but they seemed to be in a hurry. Charlotte and I stayed out of their way until they had driven off.

We decided to walk around the house again, just as we had the last time we were there. It didn't look all that different. The workmen must have still been taking things out from the inside. A couple of windows had been pulled from the walls and they were leaning against the house. The bushes around the sides looked a little beaten down where the workers had been walking. And the railing on the back porch had come loose and was hanging at a crazy angle.

"You know, Charlotte," I said, "I think all those noises we heard last time were just in our imaginations."

She looked at me. Maybe she could tell by my tone of voice that I was really just trying to convince myself — and her — that there was nothing to be scared of. "But what about the things we *saw*, Stacey?" she asked. "What about the flies, and that face at the window?"

"I'm sure there's an explanation for every-thing," I said. "Maybe those flies were actually termites." The face I wasn't so sure about. Maybe I'd just imagined that. After all, I'd been the only one to see it. That must be it. My imagination had just run away with me last Friday.

"Fire! Fire!" yelled Charlotte all of a sudden. She sounded terrified.

She was pointing toward a window on the first floor. Sure enough, flames were shooting out of it. Uh-oh. This was *not* my imagination. This was serious.

I looked around frantically. How could I put out the blaze? What if the whole house started burning? There was no hose, and even if there had been one, I didn't see any faucets on the outside of the house. Finally I saw a wheelbarrow off to the side, almost hidden in the weeds. It was full of rainwater! I ran to grab it and started to push it toward the house. Water sloshed around and spilled all over my legs, but I kept on pushing.

Charlotte had been shrieking all this time, but suddenly she stopped. I'd gotten the wheelbarrow almost up to the house. Now I looked at the window and saw that the flames had disappeared. I felt like I was going crazy. What was happening here?

My heart was pounding like mad, and I could hardly catch my breath. I set the wheelbarrow down and walked toward the window. Charlotte hung back. I looked at the empty frame. The wood wasn't charred, and the paint wasn't blistered. I didn't smell smoke. I reached up gingerly and touched the sill. It wasn't even warm. I couldn't see inside the window, but I could tell that where there once had been fire there was no fire now. The house stood silent and cold.

I turned to look at Charlotte. Her face was white and she was hugging herself as if to keep warm. "Our imaginations again?" she asked in a small voice.

I just shook my head, bewildered. Why had we ever come back to this place? Something very weird was happening here. This house was not at rest. I grabbed Charlotte's hand and walked home quickly, without looking back.

At the Baby-sitters Club meeting that afternoon, we told everybody what we'd seen, and Claud filled us in on her research. That was one meeting where not much business got done.

I tried to shut the house out of my thoughts completely for the rest of the evening, and I think Charlotte did, too. We were both pretty quiet at dinner that night, but luckily my mom didn't ask any questions. I didn't want to have to try to explain anything.

At bedtime I read to Charlotte for awhile, and then we talked. We talked about her going back to school the next day. We talked about her parents and how they'd be home in just a few days. We talked about her grandpa. We did *not* talk about the house.

When I went to bed I was still feeling pretty keyed up. I didn't think I'd ever get to sleep, but finally I drifted off. . . .

I was standing outside the old house. This time the flames shot out of every window and up through the roof. It was really burning this time. I tried to yell "Fire!" but my mouth wouldn't form the word. Then I tried to run for help, but my feet were stuck to the ground. I looked helplessly at the house and saw, to my horror, a figure at one of the windows. The person, whoever it was, clearly needed help. Again, I tried to move, but I was frozen in position. I could only watch as the person gestured to me, pleading to be rescued.

I sat bolt upright in bed. What a nightmare! My heart was beating wildly. I tried to calm myself. The dream had seemed so real. I still felt the terror of seeing that helpless person trapped in the incredible blaze. If only I could have saved him. I lay back down, but my eyes were wide open. I didn't really want to go to sleep. What if the nightmare came back?

I almost wished I were a little kid again, so I could tiptoe into my parents' room and wake up Mom. I would tell her all about my nightmare and she'd tell me it was just a bad dream and that she'd take care of me. Then I'd snuggle up in the big warm bed and go back to sleep, feeling safe. But I wasn't a little girl anymore. I was an eighth-grader who should be able to sleep alone without being scared.

I tried to think of other things, nice things. I thought of lying on a beach, the warm sun soaking into my skin. I thought of the waves crashing against the shore with a steady beat.

Bang! My door slammed open and Charlotte flew across the room. She leapt into my bed and buried herself beneath the covers. She was shaking.

"Charlotte, what is it?" I asked. "What's the matter?"

She wouldn't — or couldn't — talk at first, but slowly it began to come out. Charlotte had also had a nightmare. And hers was also about the house.

"There was a storm coming," she said, still breathing hard. "I could hear the thunder, and lightning was flashing in the sky. Then all of a sudden the ground where I was standing — right there by the house — started to shake!" She shivered. She was really frightened.

"It's okay, Charlotte," I said. "What happened then?" I knew she would feel better if she finished telling me her dream. I hugged her close and smoothed her hair.

"The ground was rumbling. It was like an earthquake or something. I thought it was going to open up and swallow me!" I don't know how she knew what an earthquake was like. Maybe she'd seen one of those nature specials on TV.

"The sky was all dark, kind of a greenish color. I was so scared, Stacey, but I couldn't move. I wanted to run, or scream, or do *something*, but all I could do was stand there and stare at the house."

I knew *that* feeling.

"Then the worst part happened. I was looking at the front of the house, and all of a sudden I saw something at the front door, or at the hole where the front door used to be. It was a pair of hands, two old, old hands. They were all skinny and bony, and they were waving at me. It was like they were saying, 'Come in, Charlotte. Come in.' Oh, Stacey! It was so awful!" She started crying for real now.

I shuddered. It sounded terrifying. I just couldn't believe it. We'd both had nightmares at the same time, and both of them were about that creepy old house.

What kind of power did that house have? What was it that drew us there at the same time that it scared us away? Had anyone else seen what we'd seen, heard what we'd heard? I suddenly realized why it was that the workmen packed up and left so early every day. It must have been the house. It had them in its power, too. Those workmen were probably just as scared as we were.

I almost had to laugh at the thought of those big men being as scared as two girls. But it wasn't really funny. I pulled the covers around Charlotte and let her snuggle up next to me. I'm sure she thought she was being allowed to stay with me because she'd been scared by that dream. She didn't know that she was as much of a comfort to me as I was to her.

CHAPTER 11

I guess Charlotte and I both managed to get back to sleep. When we woke up the next morning it was a little late, and we really had to rush to get ready for school. Charlotte couldn't wait to get back to her classes — she was tired of being home, sick.

She took her medicine (she still had to finish the bottle even though she felt fine) without too much fuss, for once. When we had raced through breakfast, my mom drove us to school so we wouldn't be late.

I don't know about Charlotte, but my day at school was not the greatest. I was sleepy from being awake in the middle of the night, but that wasn't really the problem. The problem was that I still felt totally frightened by the nightmare I'd had, and by the fact that Charlotte had had one, too. That old house was all I could think about.

I was having a hard time concentrating on

my classes. In Math, while I was supposed to be figuring out what "X" equaled, I was really thinking about flames and bony hands and swarms of flies. I don't even remember what we talked about in English class, because I wasn't listening. I was remembering that face at the window. And forget about gym class. The volleyball bounced right off my head as I stood there trying to recall exactly how that moaning had sounded.

I was a mess.

By the time lunchtime rolled around, I was dying to see my friends. I could talk to them about this. They would understand. They were all obsessed with the house, too.

I met up with Dawn on the lunch line. She and I were both picking and choosing very carefully from what was available. Dawn usually brings some kind of whole-grain stone-ground organic stuff, but she must have been running late that morning, too. We both avoided the "chicken chow mein" (gluey-looking gray stuff over noodles) and reached for fruit, milk, and plain cheese sandwiches.

"Are you okay, Stace?" she asked, as we walked over to our usual table. "You don't look so hot."

"I'm fine. I'm just a little tired, I guess," I said. "I had a terrible nightmare last night."

By that time we'd gotten to our table, and everyone else was already there. They all wanted to hear about my nightmare, so I described it in all its gruesome glory. Then I told them that Charlotte had also had a nightmare, and I repeated her scary details.

I guess they could tell that I was really frightened, because they took it seriously.

"We've got to get to the bottom of this," said Kristy. "Is there really something going on at that house? It sounds like it might be very dangerous. There are a lot of kids living in that neighborhood. What if something happened to one of them? I hereby call an emergency meeting of the Baby-sitters Club!"

Wow. We rarely have emergency meetings, and when we do, they're usually about babysitting or club problems.

"I'll be there," said Claud. "Today's art class was canceled. I can't think about anything else, anyway."

"Me, neither," said Mary Anne. "That house really gives me the creeps. And if the whole town of Stoneybrook really is built over a burial ground, just think of all the terrible things that could start happening." I knew she'd seen that Stephen King movie *Pet Sematary*. She'd let Dawn talk her into going, but afterward they were both sorry. They were probably thinking about the movie a lot these days.

Everybody agreed that an emergency meeting was a great idea. As it turned out, Jessi was the only one who wouldn't be able to make it. She had ballet class.

I felt better knowing that we were all in this together. I was able to pay a little more attention to my afternoon classes, but even so, the day seemed to drag on forever.

When school finally ended, I ran home to meet Charlotte. She'd had a rough day, too. She was thrilled to hear that an emergency club meeting had been called and that she'd been invited again.

"I'm almost like a real member now," she said.

I knew it would be a few years before Charlotte would be a sitter, but I also knew that being invited to the meeting meant a lot to her. "That's right, Char," I said. "Maybe someday you'll be president of your own baby-sitters club. You could wear a visor to every meeting, just like Kristy."

We headed over to Claudia's early, since we were both so eager for the meeting to start. I guess everybody felt the same way, because by four-thirty they were all there. Except for Jessi, of course.

Kristy called the meeting to order and announced a special agenda. "This is an emergency meeting to address the mystery of Stoneybrook, and especially to figure out what's going on at that old house. Let's go over what we know so far," she said.

"We know that there are some very weird things happening there," I said, "and that the house has — or the spirits of the people buried beneath it have — some kind of power."

"That's right," said Claud. "The power to drive us crazy!" She was sitting on her bed, chewing grape bubble gum and blowing purple bubbles, which matched her tie-dyed T-shirt dress. "I mean, really. None of us can think about anything else."

"I hear you had a nightmare last night, Charlotte," said Mary Anne. "That sounded scary."

"It was!" said Charlotte. "Those bony old hands . . . I'll never forget them."

"Tell us again about everything you saw and heard at the house," said Dawn.

Charlotte and I told the whole story once more, from faces to flies to flames. Then Kristy told us again about what she'd found in Watson's old books, and Claud repeated the stuff she'd learned at the library.

"There's something else, too," she said. "I wasn't going to tell you all, because it sounds so weird. I thought you'd think I was crazy. But I went by the old house today, just before I came here."

We all leaned forward. She looked scared, almost as if she didn't want to think about what had happened.

"I was standing there looking at the house. I wasn't even very close to it. All of a sudden, I felt a hand on my arm, but when I looked, nobody was there. It was like an invisible person was standing next to me, and he — or she — wanted my attention." Claud was being very serious. She was not kidding about this.

My mouth was hanging open. So was Charlotte's. I was glad that had never happened to me! That would have really been the last straw. Maybe we should just forget all about this house, I thought. This was getting too scary. I looked around the room. Everybody looked as scared as I felt, but they all looked fascinated, too. I knew we'd never give up now.

"What did you *do*, Claud?" asked Mary Anne.

"I ran!" said Claudia. "I wasn't about to

hang around and find out what it was they wanted from me. They probably wanted to steal my soul!"

"More likely they wanted to steal your Ding-Dongs," I said. "Even spirits like junk food."

We all laughed. I think everybody was feeling a little tense, and we just needed an excuse to giggle for awhile.

But the laughter stopped when Mallory spoke up. "You know," she said, "I just remembered something that happened to me a long time ago. It must have been last year some time. It was spring, and Vanessa and I had gone hunting for flowers together. We wanted to make a Mother's Day bouquet for our mom. We walked over to that house because I had remembered that old overgrown garden there. Sure enough, there were some really pretty flowers hidden in the weeds."

I had noticed those old flower beds. They lay along the side of the house.

"We picked the flowers and went home. My mom loved her bouquet, but that night I had the strangest nightmare." Mallory's voice was kind of dreamy. "In it, I was back at the house, staring up at it. In every window and doorway there were people, looking at me and holding out their bony hands. They didn't say anything, but I got the strongest feeling that they were angry at me for stealing their flowers. They wanted them back." She shivered. "Of course, I couldn't give them back — they'd already been picked and given to my mom. What a scary dream. I just remembered it today!"

We all sat there quietly. We'd succeeded in scaring ourselves silly. Kristy tried to calm us down.

"Maybe we're letting this get to us too much. You know, I showed Watson that map I found, and he said it's just of a *part* of Stoneybrook — the part where the cemetery is now."

"I found a map, too. Remember, Kristy?" said Claud. "And at first I thought that mine showed the same thing yours did. But you know how I am at reading maps and following directions."

Charlotte spoke up in a timid voice. "Does it really matter if the house — and the town — is built on a burial ground? Everybody's still having all these weird experiences."

As usual, Charlotte had gotten to the heart of the matter. She may be a kid, but she's sharp.

"You're right," said Kristy. "It doesn't matter at all. There are too many other strange things going on. That's why it's time to find

Mr. Ronald Hennessey and pay him a visit. Any volunteers?" She raised her own hand.

We all looked at each other. Slowly, Charlotte put up her hand, so I did, too. I had to stick with her. After all, I was her baby-sitter. Then Claud's hand crept up, too.

"That's enough," said Kristy. "We don't want to overwhelm him. He might be sick or something."

Dawn, Mary Anne, and Mallory all looked relieved. Charlotte, Kristy, and Claud looked terrified, and I'm sure I did, too.

CHAPTER 12

Wednesday

I guess if anything could take my mind off that scary old house it would be sitting for the Pikes. Even with Mallory there to help, it was like being in the middle of a three-ring circus. Maybe a circus would even be easier. I'd almost rather put my head in a lion's mouth than go through another dinner hour at the Pikes'! (Only kidding, Mal.)

That's okay, Dawn. I know it's a madhouse. But we had fun, too. You're not mad because you had to play the Wicked Witch, are you?

No way! I love being the Wicked Witch. "I'll get you, my pretty... and your little dog, too!" Hee hee hee.

It was Tuesday night, after our emergency club meeting, and Mallory and Dawn were sitting at the Pikes'. I really do like being an only child, but sometimes when I hear about an evening at the Pikes' I get a little jealous. It must be fun to have a built-in gang of friends around all the time. The Pikes are: Byron, Adam, and Jordan, the triplets, who are ten; nine-year-old Vanessa; eight-year-old Nicky; seven-year-old Margo; five-year-old Claire. And, of course, Mal, Dawn's co-baby-sitter.

Dawn arrived at six-twenty, just as Mr. and Mrs. Pike were about to leave. She'd known when she accepted the job that she and Mal would have to give the kids dinner, but she'd forgotten what dinner hour at the Pike house can be like.

Mr. and Mrs. Pike are very smart about raising a big family. They know that some things just aren't worth making a fuss about, not with eight kids to deal with. For example, meal-times. Since some kids will eat anything while others are fussy eaters, and some will eat a ton while others just pick, the Pikes have decided not to try to make many rules about what the kids do and don't have to eat. Especially when they have a sitter. When Mal is in charge, she usually just opens up the fridge and stands back. The kids rummage around, and each one finds whatever they want to eat. They call it a "smorgasbord."

That's exactly what happened on Tuesday night. Dawn did her best to help out, but she had a hard time dealing with some of the choices the kids made. Remember, Dawn is a true health-food fanatic. So how do you think she felt when Byron pulled out the bologna and a jar of grape jelly and began to make a sandwich?

"Are you sure that's what you want, Byron?" she asked faintly.

"Sure! It's my favorite," he said, carefully spreading the right amount of jelly on the bread.

When he'd finished, Dawn looked around. There was Nicky, holding a jar of peanut butter.

"Okay, Nicky. Peanut butter and jelly, right?" Dawn asked. She was relieved. This was a little more normal. But "normal" was not what Nicky had in mind.

"Nope. Peanut butter and bologna," he said. Dawn made a face, but she also made the sandwich. If that's what he wanted . . .

Adam and Jordan both wanted SpaghettiOs, but they refused to let Mal heat them up. They wanted to eat them right out of the can. She convinced them to at least put their servings on plates.

Margo just wanted bread and butter for dinner. She's in a picky phase, and there are very few foods she'll eat.

Dawn asked Vanessa what she was having.

"A fried egg will do the trick. Butter the pan, so it won't stick," said Vanessa.

Mal groaned. Was Vanessa, who longed to be a poet, going to drive them crazy by speaking in rhyme all night?

While Dawn fried the egg, Mal helped Claire get her dinner. She wanted cereal, but it had to be in a certain bowl (the one with Big Bird on it) with a certain spoon (the one with the red handle). The milk had to be poured precisely so that it came right up to the border painted inside the bowl, and no further. Finally the bowl of cereal was just right, and Claire carried it to the table.

"Thank you, Mallory-silly-billy-goo-goo!" she called over her shoulder.

"You're welcome, Claire," said Mal, rolling her eyes. It looked like Claire was in her "silly" mood again.

Mal made herself a ham sandwich, while Dawn checked the fridge for anything resembling health food. Finally she turned up a couple of carrots, a container of yogurt, and some wheat germ left over from one of Mal's baking experiments.

"This'll do just fine," she said. "Let's sit down."

There was a mad rush for the "good" seats. Claire had already claimed Mrs. Pike's usual spot, and Margo sat next to her. The triplets jostled each other, tripping and blocking as they competed for Mr. Pike's seat. While they were occupied, Nicky slipped into it. Vanessa drifted in and seated herself daintily in Adam's usual spot but was forced to move almost immediately when he sat in her lap, pretending not to see her.

Finally, everyone was seated. Dinner had begun.

"Want some SpaghettiOs, Nicky?" Adam asked.

"Sure!" he answered. His face lit up. His brothers usually only paid attention to him when they were teasing him.

"You *do*?" asked Jordan. "Don't you know they're made out of worms?"

Nicky's face fell and he went back to eating his sandwich. Byron quietly offered him a bite of his sandwich, but Nicky looked at it closely and shook his head. "Worms" had reminded him of something.

"The worms crawl in, the worms crawl out, the

worms play pinochle on your snout," he sang, looking very cheerful again.

"Ew!" cried Claire. She dropped her spoon into her cereal. Milk flew in all directions.

"C'mon, Nicky. We're trying to eat," said Mallory. She reached over with her napkin and wiped up some milk.

"Okay, how about this one?" he asked. *"I'm Popeye the sailor man, I live in a garbage can,"* he started.

Adam reached around Nicky and tapped him on the shoulder. Nicky stopped singing and whipped his head around to see Jordan, looking innocent. When he turned back to check on Adam, Jordan reached around to tap him on the other shoulder. Nicky looked like a spectator at a tennis match as Adam and Jordan took turns.

Dawn tried to distract them. "What shall we do tonight, guys?" she asked.

Everybody spoke up at once. Claire wanted to play Candy Land, the only game she's old enough for. Margo thought that sounded fine, too. The triplets voted for volleyball, except for Adam, who wanted to play dodgeball. Nicky thought it would be fun to build a tent out of blankets and play Indians.

It was Vanessa, though, who came up with

an idea that everyone liked. "Let's put on a play!" she said.

"Yea!"

"Let's do *Batman*!" said Byron. He loves to be the Joker.

"No, *Snow White*!" said Claire.

Dawn thought quickly. What could they do that would please everyone? "How about *The Wizard of Oz*?" she said, remembering what Kristy had said about how much her brothers and sisters liked that movie.

"Great choice, Dawn," said Mallory.

"I get to be the Scarecrow!" yelled Jordan.

"I get to be the Cowardly Lion!" yelled Adam.

"I get to be the Princess!" yelled Margo.

"Princess?" asked Nicky. "I don't remember any princess in that movie."

"There's always a princess, right, Mallory?" Margo looked at Mal for support.

"Sorry, not in this story," said Mallory. "But you can be the Good Witch. That's the closest thing to a princess in this play. Anyway, let's clear the table and clean up the kitchen before we get started. And anyone who's got homework has to do it first."

When everyone was ready, they had a quick meeting to assign the rest of the parts, and then everyone ran off to put together costumes.

The house was a little quieter for a few minutes while the actors and actresses dressed up. Downstairs, Mal and Dawn looked at each other and smiled.

"Well, at least we got through dinner," Dawn said.

Just then, the triplets slid down the banister, one after the other. Adam, as the Cowardly Lion, wore a yellow fringed bedspread tied around his shoulders. Jordan had on old jeans and a flannel shirt. He looked pretty good as the Scarecrow. Byron was the Tin Woodsman, and his was the hardest costume to put together. He'd found a funnel to wear as a hat, and he was carrying a toy hatchet.

The rest of the cast gathered, and Dawn and Mal were assigned parts, too. Dawn was the Wicked Witch, and Mal was the Wizard. By the time everyone was onstage, they realized that there were no people left over to be an audience, but by then it was too late.

Vanessa, as Dorothy, carried her schoolbook bag instead of a picnic basket. Nicky, who was playing Toto, trotted along beside her. Vanessa pretended to step out of a house. "Come on out, Toto, close the door. We're not in Kansas anymore," she rhymed.

"Woof, woof," said Nicky.

Claire did a short rendition of the Munchkin song, with lots of added "silly-billy-goo-goos."

Then Byron stepped out. "Hi, Dorothy! We'll come with you. Don't cry. Here are my friends, the Scarecrow and the Cowardly Lion."

"Oh, good," said Vanessa, forgetting to rhyme for once. "But how will we get to the Emerald City?"

"I'll take you in my spaceship," said Margo, as the Good Witch.

"We're off to see the Lizard!" sang Jordan.

This was getting a little off the track, but Dawn and Mal hid their smiles and went along with it. Dawn made a truly scary Wicked Witch until Claire started to cry. Then Dawn used "magic" to turn herself into another good witch.

Halfway down the Yellow Brick Road, Nicky got bored with playing Toto. After all, he had no lines except for, "Woof, woof." "Want to hear me count to one thousand by twos?" he asked. Nobody answered — they were all busy just then — so he just started in. "Two, four, six . . ."

At the end of the play, Mal, as the Wizard, solved everyone's problems. She declared that it was bedtime in Oz. Nicky had gotten up to

782 by then, but he was winding down and didn't insist on finishing.

The cast members gave themselves a big round of applause, since there was no audience to do it for them. Then Dawn took Margo, Claire, and Nicky upstairs to get ready for bed. Mal and the older kids tidied up the living room, which looked like that tornado really *had* been through it.

By the time Dawn got the younger Pikes to bed, Mr. and Mrs. Pike were home. Dawn and Mallory shook hands solemnly and congratulated each other on making it through the evening. Then Mr. Pike walked Dawn home. She breathed a huge sigh of relief as she entered her quiet old house.

CHAPTER 13

Charlotte and I got home from school at around the same time on Wednesday afternoon. I could see right away that she was as nervous as I was about going to see Mr. Hennessey.

"Are you sure you want to go, Charlotte?" I asked. "You don't *have* to do this, you know." I wondered if this thing was completely out of hand. Was I so involved with this mystery that I was forgetting to be a responsible baby-sitter?

But Charlotte, although she *was* a little scared, was also very determined to do everything she could to help solve the mystery. There was no way she was going to quit now.

We headed over to Claud's, where we'd planned to meet Kristy, who arrived at the same time we did. Claudia opened the door before we even had a chance to knock. It seemed as if we were all eager to get going, so we headed off to Stoneybrook Manor.

It took us awhile to get there — it was a longer walk than I'd thought. We didn't talk much along the way. I guess we were each busy with our own thoughts. Finally we stood on the sidewalk in front of the nursing home. It was a new-ish building, but it had a nice homey feeling about it. It was all on one story, and there were lots of pretty plants and flowers along the front and bordering the path to the main entrance. A few elderly men sat in wheelchairs on a patio area to the left, playing checkers.

After a few minutes passed with all of us just standing there, Kristy took the lead. "C'mon, you guys, let's go in," she said, and she walked up the path. The rest of us followed her. She stopped and waited for us at the front door. We walked in together, looking around the lobby. How were we supposed to find Mr. Hennessey? Then a young man stood up from the desk where he'd been sitting. "How may I help you?" he asked.

That was when I noticed the sign that a trailing plant had hidden: RECEPTION DESK. None of us said anything for a moment. I thought the man might tell us to get lost when we told him what we wanted. After all, we were just a bunch of kids. Finally, Claud spoke up.

"We're here to see a Mr. Ronald Hennessey. I understand that he is a resident here," she said. I think she was trying to sound like her heroine, Nancy Drew. The "girl detective" usually talks like that when she's on a case.

The man behind the desk gave us a big smile. "Why, how nice for Mr. Hennessey to have some young visitors," he said. He turned to a woman who was working at the desk next to his. "Ruth, can you bring Mr. Hennessey to the lounge?"

Well, this was easier than I'd thought. I looked at my fellow "detectives." Kristy seemed relieved, but Claud and Charlotte still looked nervous.

"Would you girls sign the guest register?" asked the receptionist. He gestured to a large book on a stand next to his desk. We signed in, each of us filling in our name, address, and phone number. Claud used her pink neon pen that she loves. For some reason that made me want to giggle, but I held it in. Then we walked over to the lounge area and sat down to wait. We didn't talk much. Claud fiddled with her charm bracelet, Kristy twirled her hair around a finger, and Charlotte sat and stared at the other people in the lounge until I signaled to her to stop.

After about ten minutes, Ruth reappeared, pushing an old man in a wheelchair. And when I say old, I mean *old*. He was all shriveled up — he looked about the size of a ten-year-old — and hunched over. He had a blanket over his legs, and he wore a heavy sweater, even though it didn't seem all that cool in the building. I saw hearing aids in both of his ears. His hands, the papery skin covered with brown spots, lay on his lap, picking at the blanket. But his eyes looked bright as he focused on each of us in turn. He cleared his throat and looked straight at me.

"What's your name, young lady? And what do you want with Ronald Hennessey?" His voice sounded rusty, as if he hadn't used it much lately.

"I . . . I'm . . . Stacey McGill." I finally got it out. "And these are my friends Claudia, Kristy, and Charlotte."

He nodded at each of them, but he didn't smile. He didn't seem all that delighted with his "young visitors." He looked back at me. I realized that I hadn't told him yet why we were there.

"Mr. Hennessey, we came to ask you about an old house on Elm Street. Didn't you once own it?" I asked. I figured we might as well keep on going, as long as we were there.

"Own it? Yes, I owned it. Lived there all my life. Born in the east bedroom," he said shortly. "What about it?"

"Well, we've been noticing some strange things happening there lately," I said. "Ever since they started to tear the house down."

"Oh?" he said. He was still acting grumpy, but I thought I could see a spark in his eyes all of a sudden. We'd gotten him interested. "Strange things? Like what?"

"We've heard odd noises," I said.

"And we've seen some scary things, too!" added Charlotte.

We started to tell him the story from the beginning, and I could see him perk up as he listened.

"And Charlotte and I both had awful nightmares about the house, on the same night," I told him, and then Claud chipped in her story about feeling a hand on her arm.

"I have to tell you girls that none of this surprises me," said Mr. Hennessey. "I lived in that house for almost eighty years, and I couldn't begin to tell you all the things that happened there. But I loved the house just the same. I'd never have sold it but for the fact that I know I'll never be able to live there again

119

by myself. I'm just not able to get up and down those stairs anymore."

Looking at him, we could see that it was more than just stairs that kept him from living alone. He didn't look capable of taking care of himself any longer. He was frail and tired and very, very old. But what kinds of things was he remembering about the house? I asked him to tell us more.

"Well," he said, "the very first thing I remember was when I was just a lad in short pants. I was seven or eight years old, I suppose. I woke up in the middle of the night to the sound of heavy footsteps. Someone was pacing in the corridor outside my room. I crept out of my bed and peeked through the door, which was open a crack. What a funny-looking man! He wore the strangest old-fashioned clothes, and his nose . . . well, his nose looked like it was made of rubber! I stifled a giggle, and he turned and glared at me. I drew back. I was very afraid.

"Later I learned that this man was a ghost, a ghost who went by the name of Old Rubbernose. When he was living, a horse had bitten off his nose, and the town doctor had fashioned a new one of rubber. Children laughed at Old Rubbernose, and women spurned him. He died a lonely, sad, and bitter man, and it was said that he would never rest until he found a mortal woman who would love him despite his disfigurement. He may be pacing still!"

We were all leaning forward to hear every word of his story. I was fascinated and terrified, all at the same time. Could he be telling the truth? Old Rubbernose? I looked at Claud. She raised her eyebrows. Mr. Hennessey started another story.

"And then there was the time my Uncle James came to visit. One morning he told us about a beautiful woman with red hair who was wearing a green velvet dress. She came into his room with a lit candle and bade him follow her. He got out of bed, but as he followed her out the door and down the hall, she became more and more transparent and finally disappeared. The rest of us never saw her, but every time Uncle James came to visit she would turn up. I guess she'd taken a liking to him."

That story sounded like it was out of one of those books Dawn likes to read all the time. One was called *Stories NOT to Be Read After Dark*. Was Mr. Hennessey for real?

He told us a few other stories about the house, one involving a man who carried his own head around and another about an attic door that wouldn't stay shut until a spirit was put to rest. His eyes were really sparkling now. It was obvious that he was enjoying his "young visitors" after all. Kristy caught my eye and shrugged. I knew that the others were as doubtful as I was about some of these stories. But then Mr. Hennessey said something that really grabbed our attention.

"I suppose that all of these events had a single cause," he said. "All those restless spirits . . . they were all justly unhappy because a town had been built over their graves. And if Old Rubbernose had ever killed us all in our beds, it would have been because he was angry at us for building a house right on top of his grave."

I gasped. We hadn't told Mr. Hennessey about the maps Kristy and Claud had found. Could all of his stories be true after all? None of us were able say a word. I noticed that Claud was white as a sheet.

"I think we should respect those spirits. I don't blame them one bit for being upset about having their graves disturbed," Mr. Hennessey went on. "All they want is to rest peacefully, with grass and sky over them. But then a house is built over them. And then, if that wasn't enough, the house has to be torn apart and the earth around it defiled! It's no wonder they've been reacting as they have."

"Are — are you saying that my neighborhood is *haunted?*" I asked.

"Well, missy, I can't say for sure," he answered. "But you'll know once the house is finally torn down."

That was supposed to happen the next day! What did he mean! What was going to happen?

"How will I know?" I whispered. I could hardly speak.

Mr. Hennessey wouldn't answer. Kristy, Claud, and Charlotte just sat and gaped at him. I asked him again.

He shook his head. "Sometimes people are safer not knowing," he said. "I'd stay away from that house. I don't like the sound of what you've seen and heard there." He stopped with that and wouldn't say another word about the house.

I felt frustrated and more scared than ever. But Mr. Hennessey looked tired all of a sudden, so we decided it was time to leave. I thanked him, and he nodded wearily and raised his hand in a wave. "Just be careful," he said.

Once again, we didn't get much done at our club meeting later that day. Of course we answered the phone and arranged jobs and everything — nothing gets in the way of that — but that was about it. We spent the rest of the time talking about the house, and about Mr. Hennessey's stories. Claud did a great rendition of the "Old Rubbernose" story — in fact, she really had us laughing for a few minutes. But by the time Charlotte and I walked home from the meeting, I wasn't laughing anymore. Mr. Hennessey's words echoed in my mind. "Just be careful." It was a warning.

CHAPTER 14

The next day was Thursday, the day the house was scheduled to come down. I didn't get much sleep at all on Wednesday night. Neither did Charlotte, judging by how bleary-eyed she looked at breakfast that morning. Once again I sleepwalked through all my classes that day. Maybe it was a good thing that the house was coming down at last. If this went on much longer, my grades might really suffer. Lately I just couldn't concentrate on anything but that house.

Charlotte and I had talked it over seriously and decided that we would pay attention to Mr. Hennessey's warning. We would not go and watch as the house was torn down. Maybe Mr. Hennessey was a little crazy — or senile — but it didn't matter to us. We didn't know *what* might happen when the house was knocked down, and we didn't plan to be there to find out. Our nightmares had been scary enough; we didn't need to see the real thing.

We were sitting on the front steps of my house, trying to talk about anything *but* the house, when we noticed that there seemed to be more traffic than usual on my street. Kids went by on bikes and skateboards. Moms pushed strollers. Older kids cruised by in their cars. Everybody was headed in the same direction. I guess the demolition of the old house was a major event in Stoneybrook. Everybody wanted to be there.

Including Charlotte. "Stacey, why can't we go if everybody else is going?" she asked. "Let's go. Please?"

Part of the reason I'd decided to stay home was for Charlotte's sake. I'd been behaving less than responsibly toward her, exposing her to all these scary stories and everything. At least that's how I was beginning to feel. But if she really wanted to go, maybe we should, I thought. Anyway, what could happen with such a big crowd of people around?

"Okay, Charlotte. We might as well go," I said. I took her hand and we set off down the street to join the party.

As we got closer to the house, I started to see people I knew. I saw Suzi and Buddy Barrett standing on the corner together. They waved to us. All the Pike kids were there.

126

They made a crowd all by themselves. The triplets were playing freeze tag with some other kids, and I heard Nicky teasing Claire by singing *his* version of "The Wheels on the Bus." He sang, *"The wheels on the bus go back and forth, back and forth . . ."* Then, *"The wipers on the bus go round and round, round and round . . ."* Mallory, who was keeping an eye on her brothers and sisters, made him stop when Claire started to cry.

Mary Anne was there with Jenny Prezzioso, whom she was sitting for that day. Jenny was dressed up for the occasion, which was nothing new. Jenny is *always* dressed up. She had on a white frilly dress with a pink pinafore over it. Her tights had rosebuds on them and she wore white party shoes with big pink bows on them. Charlotte stared at her while Mary Anne and I said hello. Jenny looked back at Charlotte and preened a little.

"Do you like my most beautiful new dress?" she asked coyly.

Charlotte seemed unsure of what to say, so I spoke up. "It's very nice, Jenny. I hope it won't get dirty, though, while you watch the house get torn down." Maybe someday Mrs. Prezzioso will start dressing Jenny like a normal kid.

Charlotte was waving at someone. I looked

in that direction and saw Claud, with Myriah and Gabbie in tow. They looked excited by the action. It *was* exciting. It was like a fair or something, with all these people milling around. Some adults were there, too. I saw a woman who works at the bank talking with our mailman.

Then I heard someone calling my name and turned around just in time to see Kristy drive by with her brothers Charlie and Sam. They parked, and she came over to stand with me and Charlotte.

"This is the big day, right, Stacey?" she said. "I wonder if Mr. Hennessey's stories were for real. I guess we'll know for sure soon."

Just then the workmen came out of the house. I guess they'd been making some last-minute preparations. One of them got into the operator's seat of a crane standing nearby and turned it toward the house. The big wrecking ball swung forward and crashed into the up-permost tower. This was it!

The ball kept swinging and the crowd hushed as we all watched the house start to crumble before our eyes. Charlotte held my hand tightly. The few windows that were left in the house shattered as the ball shook the building. The porch railing finally let go en-tirely and fell off into the weeds below. It wasn't long before the whole second story was gone, and it was clear that the rest of the job would go quickly. I started to calm down. It looked as though nothing were going to happen after all.

Boy, was I wrong. Just then, I saw something *very* awful. The house — what was left of it — suddenly went up in flames. The fire crackled and roared as it engulfed the wreckage. I looked around, terrified. What should we do? But everybody was just standing there, looking slightly bored. Kristy had wandered off to talk to Sam. Charlotte was watching one of the workmen pack his tools away into his truck. Nobody else seemed to see the fire!

I turned back to check again. Maybe I'd been imagining things once more. But the flames were even higher by now. Smoke curled up as the fire moved quickly through the tumbledown structure. And then, just as in my dream, I saw a figure. It was calling for help. It looked like an old, old man. Was it — could it be — Mr. Hennessey? I couldn't believe my eyes. Just as in my dream, my feet were rooted to the ground. I wanted to help, but what could I do? Then I felt Charlotte tugging on my hand.

"Let's go, Stacey," she said. "This is getting kind of boring. Nothing weird happened at all. I guess there wasn't really any mystery after all. Mr. Hennessey probably *is* just a crazy old man."

I shook my head, trying to clear my thoughts. What was going on? When I looked at the house again, there was no fire. But I had a terrible feeling in the pit of my stomach, and it had to do with Mr. Hennessey. I felt like he needed help, and like it was up to me to go to him. It was the weirdest feeling, let me tell you, but it was overwhelming and I couldn't ignore it.

I dragged Charlotte over to where Claud stood with Myriah and Gabbie. "Claud, can you watch Charlotte for a little while? I've got to go see Mr. Hennessey, right now," I said breathlessly. She must have thought I was nuts, but she just nodded. Charlotte looked up at me, confused. But there was trust in her eyes, too. I think she could see that somehow this meant a lot to me. I knelt down and gave her a hug. "Be good, Char. I'll be back soon," I said.

I took off for Stoneybrook Manor, running until I got a stitch in my side, then walking, then running some more. I still didn't understand exactly why I felt I had to go there, but the feeling was stronger than ever. It seemed to take ages to reach the home, but finally I stood on the sidewalk, just as I had yesterday, looking at Stoneybrook Manor. I took a deep breath, walked up the path, and pushed open the door. The man at the reception desk rose from his seat as I approached.

"How may I help you?" he asked, just as he had yesterday. I could see that he didn't remember me.

"I . . . I'm here to see Mr. Ronald Hennessey, please," I said. I was still breathing hard from all that running.

The man's eyes lit up. He did remember me! But then a sad look came over his face. He walked around his desk and put his hand on my shoulder. He looked straight into my eyes and said, "I'm so sorry to have to give you this unhappy news, but Mr. Hennessey passed away just last night."

CHAPTER 15

I was in shock. Mr. Hennessey was dead! I just couldn't believe it.

And I couldn't say a word. I must have looked pretty silly. Finally, someone spoke. "Aren't you Stacey McGill?" It was the woman, Ruth, who had wheeled Mr. Hennessey out to see us.

"Mr. Hennessey couldn't stop talking about you after you left," she said. "He was very pleased to make your acquaintance. He left this note for you." She pulled a folded piece of paper out of her pocket and handed it to me.

I took the note and thanked her. Then I walked over to the lounge and sat down to read it. Sure enough, my name was on the outside of the paper. *"Miss Stacey McGill"* it said, in an old-fashioned-looking script. I opened it up.

"*Dear Miss McGill,*" I read. "*I hope to be able to tell you this in person, but if for some reason I cannot, this letter will serve my purpose.*"

It was almost as if he'd known he was going to die! I read some more.

"*I enjoyed our brief meeting. You and your friends brought a moment of interest and a spark of fun to a lonely old man's life. In fact, I'm afraid that I must confess to being a bit carried away with your 'mystery.'*"

What was he saying?

"*I sincerely hope that my tall tales did not disturb you too greatly. And, to set the record straight, there was not one grain of truth in any of them! I know that children your age love a mystery, but please don't be too sad that this one is over. That old house was nothing but a lovely and comfortable home for my family and me.*"

The note went on for a few more lines, but that was his basic message. There was no mystery after all. I felt relieved, but I *was* a little sad that it was all over. And I definitely felt sad that Mr. Hennessey was gone. He seemed to have known all about what we were going through, without our even having to tell him. Plus now we'd never know the whole truth about the house.

I walked slowly out of the lobby and up the

path. The honking of a car horn made me look up. Kristy waved at me from the backseat of Charlie's car.

"We came to pick you up, Stace!" she called. "Claudia told us you were here."

I was glad to see them, and not just because I wouldn't have to walk home now. I still felt shaky, and it was good to see familiar faces and have someone to talk to. I climbed into the backseat. Charlie started the car and we drove off.

I told Kristy about Mr. Hennessey. Then I showed her the note. She read it and smiled. "I knew it," she said. "Oh, well, it was fun while it lasted."

"But Kristy, what about all the weird things that happened to me and Charlotte?" I asked. "And to Claud and Mal? We still don't know how to explain them."

"Listen to what Charlie and Sam have to say about that," she said.

It turned out that Sam and Charlie had spent some time talking with the workmen once the house was demolished. The workmen had explained the whole process they'd gone through in taking it down, and a lot of other things got explained along the way. Charlie and Sam had heard about our "mystery" from

Kristy, so they were especially interested in clearing up some of the stranger things we'd seen and heard.

"That moaning sound *was* the pipes, Stacey," said Charlie, looking at me in the rearview mirror. "The plumbing was ancient, and it took those guys forever to get it out intact. But the Historical Society insisted."

Sam turned to smile at me. "And you know that fire you and Charlotte saw? Well, there *was* one workman who stayed behind that day. He was using an acetylene torch to loosen the bathtub from its fittings. It must have been his face you saw at the window that first day, too."

Kristy was grinning. "And remember those yucky flies that reminded you of that movie?" she said. "That was a bunch of bees whose hive had been disturbed by those guys. You're lucky you didn't get stung!"

I listened to everything they said, and it was clearer and clearer that *all* the members of the Baby-sitters Club had let their imaginations work overtime. I guess we kind of enjoyed being scared. But there was still one mystery left. Why had I seen the house go up in flames when it was being knocked down? I guess I had just been imagining things again, remembering my nightmare. I decided to forget about that "fire." If I told Kristy now, she'd think I was crazy!

Kristy and I decided not to tell the others all the details that Charlie and Sam had told us. The mystery was over, but we didn't have to take all the fun out of it for everyone else!

I asked Charlie to drop me off at the Perkinses' so I could pick up Charlotte. "Thanks for the ride," I called as I hopped out.

Claud was sitting on the front porch with Gabbie, Myriah, and Charlotte. She was reading to the girls from a book of fairy tales. They all looked up as I crossed the lawn. Then Charlotte hugged me.

"Hi, Char," I said. "Ready to go?" I looked over at Claud. She looked back at me curiously, but I just shook my head slightly, so she'd know that I didn't want to talk about anything just then. We've been best friends for so long now that it doesn't take much to get an idea across.

"Thanks, Claud," I said.

Charlotte started to ask about my trip to Stoneybrook Manor, but I gave her a vague answer and then got her off the track by reminding her of what was going to happen in just a little while. "Charlotte, let's go back to my house. Guess who'll be there really soon?"

"My parents!" she yelled, remembering. "They're coming to get me today! 'Bye, Gabbie! 'Bye, Myriah! 'Bye, Claudia!" She grabbed my arm and pulled me down the street.

Charlotte and I spent the rest of the afternoon packing up her belongings. Then we played a few games of War while we waited for her parents to arrive. A couple of times she brought up the house and the "mystery," but I steered the conversation away from those topics.

We'd just gotten started on our fourth game of War (after that week I hoped I'd never play it again) when we heard a car pull into the driveway, honking. We ran to the window. Sure enough, it was the Johanssens. Charlotte tore down the stairs, flung open the front door, and raced into their arms.

"Mommy! Daddy! Guess what? I got to go to the Baby-sitters Club meetings. And we had a mystery and it was real scary! And I was sick, very sick, but now I'm all better, and Stacey took good care of me!" She was bubbling over with all her news. Charlotte was definitely proud of herself for having survived a whole week without her parents.

Dr. Johanssen and I smiled at each other over Charlotte's head. Charlotte went on chattering about the old house and the mysterious noises we'd heard and the scary things we'd seen. I helped Mr. Johanssen pack Charlotte's things into the already jammed backseat. As we juggled suitcases around to make everything fit, I quietly told him not to be concerned about Charlotte's "mystery of Stoneybrook" tales.

"We thought there was a big mystery, but there wasn't really much of one in the end," I said. "And it was scary at times, but it was *fun* scary, like a movie. I think Charlotte liked having a mystery to solve. It took her mind off missing you."

He told me that he understood. Then he thanked me for taking such good care of Charlotte. I told him it had been my pleasure. It really had, too!

Charlotte came over to give me a big hug. It was time for her to go home. I reached into my pocket and handed her a tiny package. "This is for you, Char. But don't open it until you get home," I said. It was a couple of barrettes — glow-in-the-dark barrettes! Claud had gotten a pair for her last birthday, and we'd all thought they were the coolest. I knew Charlotte would love them.

I hugged her one more time and then helped her into the backseat. Mr. Johanssen started the car and backed down the driveway. I stood and waved until they were out of sight.

When I went back into the house, it seemed awfully quiet and still. I went to the guest room. It looked neat and tidy and very empty. I missed my "little sister."

Mom and I had a quiet dinner that night. As I was finishing the dishes, the phone rang. It was Charlotte.

"I miss you, Stacey," she said. "I wish you could be here to read *Charlotte's Web* to me."

She sounded kind of sad, but I knew she must be glad to be home with her parents, too. She told me that she loved the barrettes, and that she planned to wear them to school the next day. She told me all about her grandpa and how much better he was feeling. We talked for a long time, and we didn't mention our "mystery" once. Finally, it was time to say good-bye.

"I have to go to bed now, Stacey," said Charlotte. "Good night, big sister!"

I had a lump in my throat, but I smiled and said, "Good night, little sister. Love ya!"

Dear Reader,

I have loved scary stories ever since I was little. I always headed straight for the mystery section of our library, and each summer I read mystery after mystery. I especially liked the scary Nancy Drew titles, and I wanted to solve a mystery myself. Unfortunately, I never stumbled upon a mystery to solve like Stacey in *Stacey and the Mystery of Stoneybrook*.

Even now I like to read scary books and see scary movies. Sometimes I look away when the movie gets really scary, but I still love it. I live in a very old house out in the country, and people always ask me if it's haunted. I haven't seen a ghost yet, but I'm always on the lookout.

Happy reading,

Ann M. Martin

L. GODWIN

Ann M. Martin

About the Author

ANN MATTHEWS MARTIN was born on August 12, 1955. She grew up in Princeton, NJ, with her parents and her younger sister, Jane.

Although Ann used to be a teacher and then an editor of children's books, she's now a full-time writer. She gets the ideas for her books from many different places. Some are based on personal experiences. Others are based on childhood memories and feelings. Many are written about contemporary problems or events.

All of Ann's characters, even the members of the Baby-sitters Club, are made up. (So is Stoneybrook.) But many of her characters are based on real people. Sometimes Ann names her characters after people she knows, other times she chooses names she likes.

In addition to the Baby-sitters Club books, Ann Martin has written many other books for children. Her favorite is *Ten Kids, No Pets* because she loves big families and she loves animals. Her favorite Baby-sitters Club book is *Kristy's Big Day*. (By the way, Kristy is her favorite baby-sitter!)

Ann M. Martin now lives in New York with her cats, Gussie and Woody. Her hobbies are reading, sewing, and needlework — especially making clothes for children.

THE BABY-SITTERS CLUB

Notebook Pages

This Baby-sitters Club book belongs to _____ .

I am _____ years old and in the _____

grade.

The name of my school is _____ .

I got this BSC book from _____ .

I started reading it on _____ and

finished reading it on _____ .

The place where I read most of this book is _____ .

My favorite part was when _____ .

If I could change anything in the story, it might be the part when

_____ .

My favorite character in the Baby-sitters Club is _____ .

The BSC member I am most like is _____

because _____ .

If I could write a Baby-sitters Club book it would be about ____

_____ .

#35 Stacey and the Mystery of Stoneybrook

Stacey and the other members of the Baby-sitters Club think the Hennessey house is one of the spookiest places in their neighborhood. The spookiest place in my neighborhood is _____ _____. I think this place is spooky because _____ _____. Stacey is lucky to have her friends around to help her solve the haunted house mystery. If I were solving a mystery, the people I'd want helping me are _____ _____. I would choose these people because _____ _____. The biggest mystery I've ever tried to solve is _____ _____. This is what I did when I tried to solve it: _____ _____. Mallory has nightmares about the haunted Hennessey house. The places I have nightmares about are: _____ _____.

STACEY'S

Here I am, age three.

Me with Charlot[
my "almos[

A family portrait — me
with my parents.

SCRAPBOOK

Johanssen,
sister."

Getting ready for school.

In LUV at Shadow Lake.

Illustrations by Angelo Tillery

Read all the books
about **Stacey**
in the Baby-sitters Club series
by Ann M. Martin

The best friends you'll ever have!

Collect 'em all!

by Ann M. Martin

More titles... ▶

The Baby-sitters Club titles continued...

❏ MG48222-X	#78	Claudia and the Crazy Peaches	$3.50
❏ MG48223-8	#79	Mary Anne Breaks the Rules	$3.50
❏ MG48224-6	#80	Mallory Pike, #1 Fan	$3.50
❏ MG48225-4	#81	Kristy and Mr. Mom	$3.50
❏ MG48226-2	#82	Jessi and the Troublemaker	$3.50
❏ MG48235-1	#83	Stacey vs. the BSC	$3.50
❏ MG48228-9	#84	Dawn and the School Spirit War	$3.50
❏ MG48236-X	#85	Claudi Kishli, Live from WSTO	$3.50
❏ MG48227-0	#86	Mary Anne and Camp BSC	$3.50
❏ MG48237-8	#87	Stacey and the Bad Girls	$3.50
❏ MG22872-2	#88	Farewell, Dawn	$3.50
❏ MG22873-0	#89	Kristy and the Dirty Diapers	$3.50
❏ MG22874-9	#90	Welcome to the BSC, Abby	$3.50
❏ MG22875-1	#91	Claudia and the First Thanksgiving	$3.50
❏ MG22876-5	#92	Mallory's Christmas Wish	$3.50
❏ MG22877-3	#93	Mary Anne and the Memory Garden	$3.99
❏ MG22878-1	#94	Stacey McGill, Super Sitter	$3.99
❏ MG45575-3		Logan's Story Special Edition Readers' Request	$3.25
❏ MG47118 X		Logan Bruno, Boy Baby oltter Special Edition Readers' Request	$3.50
❏ MG47756-0		Shannon's Story Special Edition	$3.50
❏ MG47686-6		The Baby-sitters Club Guide to Baby-sitting	$3.25
❏ MG47314-X		The Baby-sitters Club Trivia and Puzzle Fun Book	$2.50
❏ MG48400-1		BSC Portrait Collection: Claudia's Book	$3.50
❏ MG22864-1		BSC Portrait Collection: Dawn's Book	$3.50
❏ MG48399-4		BSC Portrait Collection: Stacey's Book	$3.50
❏ MG47151-1		The Baby-sitters Club Chain Letter	$14.95
❏ MG48295-5		The Baby-sitters Club Secret Santa	$14.95
❏ MG45074-3		The Baby-sitters Club Notebook	$2.50
❏ MG44783-1		The Baby-sitters Club Postcard Book	$4.95

Available wherever you buy books...or use this order form.

Scholastic Inc., P.O. Box 7502, 2931 E. McCarty Street, Jefferson City, MO 65102

Please send me the books I have checked above. I am enclosing $_____
(please add $2.00 to cover shipping and handling). Send check or money order—no cash or
C.O.D.s please.

Name _____ Birthdate_____

Address _____

City_____ State/Zip _____

Please allow four to six weeks for delivery. Offer good in the U.S. only. Sorry, mail orders are not available
to residents of Canada. Prices subject to change.

THE BABY-SITTERS CLUB®

by Ann M. Martin

Collect and read these exciting BSC Super Specials, Mysteries, and Super Mysteries along with your favorite Baby-sitters Club books!

BSC Super Specials

❏ BBK44240-6	Baby-sitters on Board! Super Special #1	$3.95
❏ BBK44239-2	Baby-sitters' Summer Vacation Super Special #2	$3.95
❏ BBK43973-1	Baby-sitters' Winter Vacation Super Special #3	$3.95
❏ BBK42493-9	Baby-sitters' Island Adventure Super Special #4	$3.95
❏ BBK43575-2	California Girls! Super Special #5	$3.95
❏ BBK43576-0	New York, New York! Super Special #6	$3.95
❏ BBK44963-X	Snowbound! Super Special #7	$3.95
❏ BBK44969-X	Baby-sitters at Shadow Lake Super Special #8	$3.95
❏ BBK45661-X	Starring The Baby-sitters Club! Super Special #9	$3.95
❏ BBK45674-1	Sea City, Here We Come! Super Special #10	$3.95
❏ BBK47015-9	The Baby-sitters Remember Super Special #11	$3.95
❏ BBK48308-0	Here Come the Bridesmaids! Super Special #12	$3.95

BSC Mysteries

❏ BAI44084-5	#1 Stacey and the Missing Ring	$3.50
❏ BAI44085-3	#2 Beware Dawn!	$3.50
❏ BAI44799-8	#3 Mallory and the Ghost Cat	$3.50
❏ BAI44800-5	#4 Kristy and the Missing Child	$3.50
❏ BAI44801-3	#5 Mary Anne and the Secret in the Attic	$3.50
❏ BAI44961-3	#6 The Mystery at Claudia's House	$3.50
❏ BAI44960-5	#7 Dawn and the Disappearing Dogs	$3.50
❏ BAI44959-1	#8 Jessi and the Jewel Thieves	$3.50
❏ BAI44958-3	#9 Kristy and the Haunted Mansion	$3.50

More titles ➡

The Baby-sitters Club books continued...

What's the scoop with Dawn, Kristy, Mallory, and the other girls?

Be the first to know with G★I★R★L★ magazine!

Hey, Baby-sitters Club readers! Now you can be the first on the block to get in on the action of G★I★R★L★ It's an exciting new magazine that lets you dig in and read...

★ Upcoming selections from Ann Martin's Baby-sitters Club books
★ Fun articles on handling stress, turning dreams into great careers, making and keeping best friends, and much more
★ Plus, all the latest on new movies, books, music, and sports!

To get in on the scoop, just cut and mail this coupon today. And don't forget to tell all your friends about G★I★R★L★ magazine!

A neat offer for you...6 issues for only $15.00.

Sign up today -- this special offer ends July 1, 1996!

❏ **YES!** Please send me G★I★R★L★ magazine. I will receive six fun-filled issues for only $15.00. Enclosed is a check (no cash, please) made payable to G★I★R★L★ for $15.00.

Just fill in, cut out, and mail this coupon with your payment of $15.00 to: G★I★R★L★, c/o Scholastic Inc., 2931 East McCarty Street, Jefferson City, MO 65101.

Name _____

Address _____

City, State, ZIP _____

9013